P9-DCL-762

Seafood

THE KNAPP PRESS
Publishers
Los Angeles

Bon Appétit® is a registered trademark of Bon Appétit Publishing Corp. Used with permission.

Copyright © 1983 by Knapp Communications Corporation

Published by The Knapp Press
5900 Wilshire Boulevard, Los Angeles, California 90036

All rights reserved. No part of this book may be reproduced, stored in a retrieval system
or transmitted, in any form or by any means, electronic, mechanical, photocopying,
recording or otherwise, without permission in writing from the publisher.

Library of Congress Cataloging in Publication Data

Main entry under title:

Cooking with Bon appétit.

    Includes index.
    1. Seafood. I. Bon appétit. II. Title: Seafood.
TX747.C763 1983   641.6'9   83-9828
ISBN 0-89535-120-X

On the cover: *Mediterranean Stir-Fry*

Printed and bound in the United States of America

10   9   8   7   6   5   4   3   2

❦ Contents

Foreword . . . . *vii*

1 Crustaceans *1*
Crab 2
Shrimp 8
Lobster 23
Mixed Crustaceans 26

2 Mollusks *29*
Clams 30
Mussels 33
Oysters 39
Scallops 43
Miscellaneous Mollusks 54

3 Saltwater Fish *57*
Bass 58
Snapper 60
Sole 66
Swordfish 76
Tuna 78
Miscellaneous Saltwater Fish 79

4 Freshwater Fish *85*
Salmon 86
Salmon Trout 93

Trout 95
Miscellaneous Freshwater Fish 99

5 Basic and Mixed Dishes 101
Index 115

❧ *Foreword*

Seafood. What other ingredients are so delicious unadorned, yet also make perfect foils for countless sauces? What else is so quickly and easily prepared, yet has a flavor that shows no signs of weakening under the long, slow cooking required of a spicy stew? On its own, seafood is a star of the highest caliber, simply and briefly broiled or poached, and perhaps accented with a light squeeze of lemon and some salt and pepper. But when the technique is more complex and the seasonings more intricate— a mousse of shrimp scented with fresh dill and served with a lemony cream sauce (page 12), for example—the fine flavor of fresh seafood still steals the show.

The recipes in this book have been gathered from the pages of *Bon Appétit* and organized into chapters by the type of seafood they feature, to make a simple task of locating recipes for whatever fish is freshest at your market. The first chapter deals with Crustaceans, offering recipes for crab, shrimp and lobster. Maryland Eastern Shore Crab Cakes (page 4), crisply fried patties of seasoned crab, is one featured dish, along with such elegant fare as Lobster-Stuffed Cabbage with Chive Butter (page 23), delicate packages of savoy cabbage leaves filled with lobster and a pike mousseline. In the chapter on Mollusks, you'll find a selection as diverse as the shellfish themselves, ranging from appetizer recipes such as Grilled Oysters with Ginger-Lime Dressing (page 39) to such colorful main courses as Scallops Provençale with Pasta and Avocado (page 53).

The wide variety of recipes is enhanced by special boxed features that offer detailed information about many of the basics of cooking with seafood. There is a section, for example, on poaching fish that includes basic recipes for the poaching liquid, hints for garnishes and freezing tips. Another feature, Sashimi and Sushi, tells you all about these Japanese creations— how they are made and what they are made of. And all the classic sauces for fish are here for your convenience.

Other features range from a traditional clambake to a discussion on the best wines to select for your fish dinner. Handy and practical, classic yet innovative, this volume brings the best of fresh, tempting seafood to you, your family and your friends.

1 ❧ Crustaceans

Crustaceans are among the most sought after and popular of all seafood. For many, the inclusion of crab, shrimp and lobster in a menu elevates the meal to a special occasion.

All of these favorites—from hors d'oeuvres to main courses; for brunch, lunch or dinner—can be found in this chapter. Recipes include casual easy-to-make Crab Puffs Supreme (page 2) and Baked Prawns with Garlic and Herbs (page 16) and more elegant fare like Shrimp Mousse with Sauce Nantua (page 12), Terrine of Crab with Fresh Vegetables (page 4) or Hot Sherried Lobster in Brioche (page 25). Down-home cooks will want to try Maryland's Eastern Shore Crab Cakes (page 4), Carolina Pickled Shrimp (page 9), Dockside Murphy's Crab Stew (page 7) or New Orleans-style Shrimp Etouffée (page 17) with its zesty wine-enhanced sauce. Crocked Shrimp and Cheese with Cucumber Rounds (page 9) transforms a single pound of shrimp into an inexpensive party spread for ten.

And there is also an array of ethnic specialties from which to choose. Crab in Black Bean Sauce (page 7), Coconut Shrimp Balls (page 8) and Gingered Prawns (page 17) have a definite oriental flair. From India comes a pair of superb curries: Seafood Cream served with aromatic Cinnamon Rice (page 28) and Shrimp Korma (page 21). Seafood in Phyllo (page 27), Scampi alla Buongustaia (page 18) and Simple Greek Shrimp (page 18) all capture the sunny flavors of the Mediterranean, while Ragoût of Lobster with Morels (page 25) comes straight from the kitchens of France's revolutionary nouvelle cuisine.

When buying shrimp and prawns in supermarkets or specialty stores to use in these recipes, look for those that are firm to the touch and somewhat green-gray in color, although the color may vary in some areas of the country. Lobsters are sold live, and should be cooked as soon after purchase as possible (the cooked meat can be frozen up to one month if desired). No matter what shrimp, prawns, crab or lobster you select, make certain it has been stored on ice and is free of any strong odor.

Cooks all over the world have relied on this trio of savory shellfish for centuries—for lusty soups and casseroles, simple sautés and fancier creations. We hope these recipes help expand your repertoire: Their appeal is timeless and their flavor superb.

🍎 *Crab*

Crab Puffs Supreme

Makes 4 dozen

1 6½-ounce can crabmeat, drained and flaked
½ cup grated sharp cheddar cheese
3 green onions, chopped
1 teaspoon Worcestershire sauce
1 teaspoon dry mustard

1 cup water
½ cup (1 stick) butter
¼ teaspoon salt
1 cup flour
4 eggs

Preheat oven to 400°F. Combine first 5 ingredients in medium bowl and mix well.

Combine water, butter and salt in large saucepan and bring to boil. Remove from heat and immediately add flour, beating until mixture leaves sides of pan and forms ball. Add eggs, one at a time, beating thoroughly after each addition. Thoroughly blend in crab mixture. Drop by small teaspoonfuls onto ungreased baking sheet. Bake 15 minutes. Reduce heat to 350°F; bake 10 minutes more.

Unbaked puffs can be frozen on baking sheet and transferred to plastic bags. Reheat without thawing at 375°F until crisp.

Umberto's Dungeness Crab

4 servings

8 crabs in shells (preferably fresh)
1 pound fresh spinach, stems removed
2 teaspoons butter
1 large onion, finely chopped
2 garlic cloves, chopped
⅛ teaspoon freshly grated nutmeg
Salt and freshly ground pepper
8 thin lemon wedges

½ cup dry white wine (preferably Frascati or other Italian wine)
1 tablespoon chopped fresh parsley
¼ cup béchamel sauce
½ cup freshly grated Parmesan cheese

If using fresh crabs, drop head first into a large amount of rapidly boiling salted water over high heat. Return water to boil. Cook crabs until very tip of leg pulls off easily without meat, about 15 minutes. Let stand under cold running water until cool enough to handle. Carefully remove meat from shells, cut into chunks and set aside. Wash shells and legs thoroughly.

Cook spinach in rapidly boiling water until just blanched, about 3 minutes. Drain well and pat dry with paper towels. Chop spinach coarsely. Melt 1 teaspoon butter in medium skillet over medium heat. Add spinach and sauté briefly. Stir in onion, garlic, nutmeg, salt and pepper. Add four lemon wedges and cook 5 minutes longer. Discard lemon.

Preheat oven to 450°F. Divide spinach mixture among four shells, spreading evenly to form a bed. Melt remaining butter in large skillet over medium heat. Add crab and sauté briefly. Stir in wine and parsley, mixing well. Arrange crab mixture over spinach. Top each with 1 tablespoon béchamel. Sprinkle Parmesan over. Bake until tops are crisp and golden, 7 to 10 minutes.

Just before serving, top each crab with extra shell. Arrange legs around shell to resemble crab and garnish with the remaining lemon wedges.

Crab Rangoon

Makes 2½ to 3 dozen

½ pound fresh crabmeat, drained and chopped
½ pound cream cheese, room temperature
½ teaspoon steak sauce
¼ teaspoon garlic powder

2½ to 3 dozen won ton wrappers
1 egg yolk, well beaten

Oil for deep frying
Chinese mustard and/or red sauce

Combine crabmeat with cream cheese and seasonings in medium bowl and blend to a paste. Place heaping teaspoon on each won ton. Gather four corners of won ton together at top. Moisten edges with egg yolk and pinch or twist together gently to seal.

Heat oil in wok, deep fryer or electric skillet to 375°F. Add won tons in batches and fry until golden brown, about 3 minutes. Remove with slotted spoon and drain on paper towels. Serve hot and accompany with Chinese mustard and red sauce for dipping.

Deviled Crab

2 servings

1 tablespoon butter
¾ cup milk
¼ cup cracker crumbs
2 eggs, lightly beaten
1 teaspoon prepared horseradish
¾ teaspoon dry mustard

2 to 4 dashes hot pepper sauce
Salt and freshly ground pepper
1 7½-ounce can crabmeat, rinsed, well drained and broken up
Melted butter

Preheat oven to 375°F. Melt butter in small skillet over medium heat. Stir in milk and cracker crumbs and bring to boil. Remove from heat and add eggs, horseradish, mustard, hot pepper sauce, salt and pepper. Blend in crabmeat. Spoon into individual ramekins or baking dish. Brush with melted butter and bake until lightly browned and heated through, about 20 minutes.

Stuffed Crab

4 servings

¼ cup (½ stick) butter
¾ cup chopped onion
½ cup chopped green onion
1 hard-cooked egg, mashed
2 cups crabmeat
½ cup half and half
¼ cup minced fresh parsley
3 garlic cloves, minced

½ teaspoon salt
¼ teaspoon freshly ground pepper
Hot pepper sauce
½ cup seasoned breadcrumbs
2 tablespoons Sherry
4 teaspoons fresh lemon juice
Butter

Preheat oven to 400°F. Melt butter in large skillet over medium heat. Add onions and cook until soft. Remove from heat and add egg, crab, half and half, parsley, garlic, salt, pepper, pepper sauce and half the breadcrumbs and stir well. Return to heat and cook about 5 minutes. Remove from heat and stir in Sherry. Stuff into 4 crab shells (or divide among ramekins). Adjust seasoning. Sprinkle with remaining breadcrumbs and lemon juice. Top each with pat of butter. Bake until tops are golden brown. Serve hot or cold.

Maryland Eastern Shore Crab Cakes

4 to 6 servings

¼ cup cracker meal
¼ cup mayonnaise
1 egg, lightly beaten
1 tablespoon minced onion
¼ teaspoon Worcestershire sauce
¼ teaspoon dry mustard
   Dash of Old Bay Seasoning*

1 pound large lump crabmeat, coarsely shredded
½ cup (1 stick) butter
½ cup breadcrumbs

Combine cracker meal, mayonnaise, egg, onion and seasonings. Pour over crab and toss gently. Heat butter in large skillet. Form crab into 4 to 6 patties and roll in breadcrumbs. Fry until golden brown.

*Available in specialty food stores.

Terrine of Crab and Fresh Vegetables
(Crabe en Terrine de Primeurs)

6 to 8 servings

¾ pound lump crabmeat including 4 legs, squeezed to remove excess liquid
1 tomato, peeled, seeded and chopped (reserve all liquid)
3 tablespoons small peas, parboiled, drained and patted dry
3 tablespoons julienne of carrot, parboiled, drained and patted dry
3 tablespoons julienne of green beans, parboiled, drained and patted dry
2 tablespoons julienne of roasted and peeled red bell pepper, patted dry
1 tablespoon fresh lemon juice or to taste
½ bunch fresh tarragon or ½ teaspoon dried, crumbled
1½ teaspoons minced fresh chives
1 parsley sprig, minced

3 tablespoons fresh cilantro (also known as coriander or Chinese parsley), leaves only

1 tablespoon unflavored gelatin
¼ cup mayonnaise
½ cup whipping cream, whipped
2 extra-large egg whites, stiffly beaten

   Pimiento Sauce (see following recipe)

Make sure crab and vegetables are as dry as possible and at room temperature. Oil 1-quart glass loaf pan; set aside. Combine crab (except legs), tomato, peas, carrot, green beans, red pepper, lemon juice, tarragon, chives, parsley and cilantro in warmed large bowl.

Combine gelatin and liquid from tomato and briefly set over hot water to soften. Add to crab mixture with mayonnaise and combine gently. Taste and adjust seasoning (mixture should be highly seasoned at this point). Fold in whipped cream and egg whites. Taste and adjust seasoning again.

Turn ⅓ of vegetable mixture into prepared pan. Arrange 2 sliced crab legs over top. Repeat, ending with vegetable mixture. Cover and chill thoroughly.

To serve, unmold loaf onto platter and cut into slices about ½ inch thick. Transfer to serving plates and carefully spoon Pimiento Sauce around slices.

Pimiento Sauce

Sauce is also good over poached salmon.

4 canned whole pimientos *or* 2 red bell peppers, roasted, peeled and seeded
2 tomatoes, peeled, seeded and drained
¼ cup olive oil

2 tablespoons fresh lemon juice
Salt and freshly ground white pepper
Hot pepper sauce
Whipping cream (optional)

Combine pimiento or peppers and tomatoes in processor or blender and mix until smooth. With machine running, alternately add olive oil and lemon juice drop by drop and mix until emulsified. Season to taste with salt, white pepper and hot pepper sauce. Strain. Cover and refrigerate until ready to serve. Thin sauce with cream, if desired.

Sautéed Crab Claws (Cua Ram Muoi)

6 to 8 servings

1 pound crab claws or king crab legs
1 teaspoon salt
Freshly ground pepper

3 tablespoons oil

4 garlic cloves, chopped
1 tablespoon tomato paste
Boston or Bibb lettuce leaves

Sprinkle crab with salt and pepper and let stand for 15 minutes.

Heat oil in large skillet over medium-high heat. Add garlic and sauté briefly. Stir in tomato paste. Add crab and stir (or shake pan) to coat crab thoroughly with sauce. Spoon onto lettuce-lined platter and serve immediately.

Baked Crab Jockey

4 to 6 servings

2 tablespoons (¼ stick) butter
3 large shallots, finely chopped
2 teaspoons curry powder
10 ounces fresh crabmeat
Dash of Worcestershire sauce
Salt and freshly ground pepper

¾ cup Velouté de Poisson (see following recipes)
¼ cup Hollandaise Sauce (see following recipes)
¼ cup whipping cream, whipped

Preheat broiler. Melt butter in medium skillet over medium-high heat until light brown. Stir in shallot and curry powder. Increase heat to high, add crabmeat and sauté about 1 minute. Blend in Worcestershire sauce, salt and pepper. Gently stir in velouté, hollandaise and whipped cream, being careful not to break up crabmeat. Transfer mixture to individual scallop shells or small broilerproof dishes. Broil until top is golden and serve.

Velouté de Poisson

Makes 1½ cups

3 tablespoons butter
¼ cup finely chopped onion
3 tablespoons all purpose flour
2 cups hot Fish Fumet (see following recipes)
3 white peppercorns

1 parsley sprig
¼ celery stalk, thinly sliced
¼ teaspoon salt
Pinch of freshly grated nutmeg

For roux, melt butter in nonaluminum medium saucepan over low heat. Add onion and cook until soft but not browned. Remove from heat and whisk in flour. Cook, whisking constantly, until roux is frothy and free of lumps, about 2 to 3 minutes. Remove saucepan from heat and slowly add half of hot fish fumet, whisking constantly. Add remaining fish fumet and continue whisking until sauce is smooth, about 3 to 5 minutes. Place over medium-low heat and add remaining ingredients. Simmer, uncovered, stirring frequently with wooden spoon, until sauce is reduced by about ¼, about 20 to 30 minutes. Strain velouté before using.

Hollandaise Sauce

Makes about 1 cup

⅓ cup water
1 teaspoon fresh lemon juice
¼ teaspoon salt
¼ teaspoon freshly ground white pepper
3 egg yolks, beaten

1¾ cups (3½ sticks) unsalted butter, melted
Pinch of ground red pepper (optional)
1½ tablespoons whipping cream

Combine water, lemon juice, salt and pepper in small saucepan and cook over high heat until reduced to 2 tablespoons. Let cool.

Place over low heat, add egg yolks and whisk constantly until mixture is thick and lemon colored; *do not overcook or yolks will curdle.* Reduce heat to lowest setting and add butter 2 tablespoons at a time, thoroughly incorporating after each addition. Blend in pepper. Stir in cream to thin to desired consistency.

Fish Fumet

Makes about 1 quart

1 pound (about) fish trimmings (do not use salmon)
1 quart cold water
2 tablespoons tarragon vinegar
1 celery stalk (with leaves), cut into 2-inch pieces
1 carrot, cut into 2-inch pieces
1 leek (white part only), split

¼ medium head of lettuce
5 white peppercorns
3 fresh dill sprigs
1 bay leaf
½ teaspoon dried thyme, crumbled
½ teaspoon salt

Combine all ingredients in 4- to 5-quart saucepan and bring to boil over medium-high heat. Reduce heat and simmer, uncovered, about 45 minutes. Strain through colander or cheesecloth-lined strainer before using.

Gabby Crabby (Hot Crab Sandwich)

6 servings, 2 open-face sandwiches per serving

1¼ pounds king crabmeat, cut into large pieces
1¼ cups mayonnaise
2 to 3 green onions, chopped
½ head iceberg lettuce, chopped
1 tablespoon seasoning salt
½ tablespoon fresh lemon juice

12 tomato slices (about 2 large tomatoes)
6 English muffins, split, toasted and buttered
12 slices mozzarella cheese (about 9 ounces)

Preheat oven to 350°F. Mix crab, mayonnaise, onion, lettuce, salt and lemon juice.

Place tomato slice on each muffin half. Arrange crab salad on top of tomato, dividing equally among sandwiches. Top each with slice of mozzarella.

Transfer sandwiches to baking sheet and bake 15 to 20 minutes, or until cheese is lightly browned.

Crab in Black Bean Sauce

6 servings

2 large green bell peppers, sliced lengthwise into ¼-inch strips
2 medium onions, sliced
1 tablespoon minced garlic
1 tablespoon fermented black beans,* rinsed and dried

1 tablespoon sugar
1 tablespoon soy sauce
1 tablespoon oyster sauce

1 tablespoon Chinese wine* (saké or pale dry Sherry may be substituted)
1½ teaspoons salt
Freshly ground white pepper

Oil for deep frying
3 large fresh crabs, boiled, cracked into pieces and well dried**
½ cup cornstarch

Combine first 4 ingredients in bowl.

In separate bowl blend sugar, soy sauce, oyster sauce, wine, salt and pepper.

Heat oil in wok to 375°F for deep frying. Meanwhile, lightly coat crab pieces with cornstarch. Deep fry a few pieces at a time, cooking each batch about 1 minute. Drain well on paper towels. Remove all but 1 or 2 tablespoons of oil from the wok.

To stir-fry: Set wok over high heat 30 seconds, swirling to coat sides and bottom with oil. When light haze forms add pepper mixture and stir-fry 1 to 2 minutes. Immediately add crab and soy sauce mixture. Stir-fry 2 minutes. Serve on heated platter.

*Available in oriental markets.
**To cook live crab, drop crab head first into large amount of rapidly boiling salted water over high heat. Return water to boil. Cook crab until very tip of leg pulls off easily without meat, about 15 minutes. Let cool before cracking into serving pieces.

Dockside Murphy's Maryland Crab Stew

Makes about 1 gallon

3 slices bacon, cut into ½-inch pieces
2½ pounds onions, chopped
1 pound carrots, peeled and chopped
1 pound celery, chopped
3 medium-size green bell peppers, seeded and diced
1½ pounds tomatoes, diced and crushed
Pinch of granulated garlic
Pinch of salt and freshly ground pepper
1½ gallons hot water
¼ cup chicken stock base

1 10-ounce can whole clams, undrained
3 medium potatoes, peeled and diced
½ cup plus 2 tablespoons Worcestershire sauce
2 tablespoons fresh lemon juice
Pinch of Old Bay Seasoning*
1½ pounds crabmeat

Sauté bacon in large saucepan or Dutch oven until crisp. Add onion, carrot, celery and green peppers and sauté until lightly golden, about 10 to 15 minutes. Add tomatoes, garlic, salt and pepper. Gradually stir in hot water, chicken stock base and clams until combined. Simmer 3 to 4 hours, uncovered, stirring occasionally.

Add potatoes, Worcestershire, lemon juice and seasoning and simmer ½ hour longer. Add crabmeat and heat through. Serve hot.

*Available in specialty food stores.

🦐 Wine With Seafood

"White wine with fish; red wine with meat" is a simple answer to a very complicated question. But it raises more questions than it answers. Is there no instance when a red wine might be a more fitting complement to seafood? Should the same wine be served with oysters as with sole?

It is too much of a simplification to group all seafood together and then make a wine recommendation accordingly. You wouldn't lump all meat or even all beef dishes together and pick just one wine—or even one type of wine—for all. Why do it with fish?

There are thousands of species of seafood, each with its own characteristics of flavor and texture. Add to this an infinite number of preparation methods and sauces, and the wine choice becomes very confounding. Actually, common sense is all that is necessary to guide you unerringly to an appropriate wine selection, so long as you steer clear of sweet wines.

The key to blissful wine and food marriages is balance. Pick rich wines to go with rich dishes, lighter wines to accompany light dishes. For instance, to complement the mild flavors of grilled white fish—such as halibut, swordfish, or sole—choose a crisp, dry Johannisberg Riesling or a light-bodied Chardonnay from France or California. The same fish varieties sautéed in butter would be best with a heavier Chardonnay.

Oilier fish, such as tuna or trout, should be matched with wines that have strong personalities and a good, snappy acidity to balance the heaviness of the seafood. White Bordeaux or Sauvignon Blanc is the ideal wine here. These same wines go best with the flavor of raw oysters and clams, which also work well with crisp Chardonnays, Muscadets, and Chablis.

And what about red wines? Light reds such as Beaujolais, Gamay or young Zinfandel are quite appropriate with heavier seafood, especially salmon. Serve them slightly chilled. Also, if red wine is used in the preparation of the dish it is appropriate as an accompaniment.

In general, your own sense of proportion and style should be enough to assure a balanced food and wine combination. Whichever you may choose, both the wine and the food will benefit from its association with the other.

🦐 Shrimp

Coconut Shrimp Balls (Perkedel Udang)

Makes about 30

1 pound uncooked shrimp, shelled and deveined

2 eggs
¼ cup grated fresh coconut
1 tablespoon cornstarch

1 teaspoon ground coriander
½ teaspoon salt

1 cup peanut oil or corn oil

Coarsely grind shrimp in processor or chop by hand. Transfer to medium bowl. Blend in eggs. Add coconut, cornstarch, coriander and salt and mix well. Refrigerate shrimp mixture for 30 minutes.

Heat oil in wok or heavy large skillet over medium-high heat. Add shrimp mixture to oil by heaping teaspoons (do not crowd) and cook until lightly browned, turning occasionally, about 3 minutes. Remove with slotted spoon and drain on paper towel. Repeat with remaining shrimp mixture. Transfer shrimp balls to platter and serve immediately.

Carolina Pickled Shrimp

6 to 8 appetizer servings

½ cup vegetable oil
⅓ cup catsup
⅓ cup white vinegar
2 tablespoons Worcestershire sauce
2 teaspoons sugar
1 teaspoon salt
½ teaspoon dry mustard
Dash of hot pepper sauce

1 pound shrimp, cooked and shelled
2 small red onions, thinly sliced
2 bay leaves, crushed

Combine first 8 ingredients and blend well. Layer shrimp, onion and bay leaves in bowl. Pour dressing over. Cover and chill at least 12 hours before serving.

Shrimp Lamaze

Serve on crackers or toast points.

6 to 8 servings

2 hard-cooked eggs, finely chopped
1 cup mayonnaise (preferably homemade)
¾ cup chili sauce
3 tablespoons India relish
1½ tablespoons minced pimiento
1½ teaspoons finely chopped green bell pepper
1½ teaspoons finely chopped celery
1 teaspoon mild prepared mustard

1 teaspoon Worcestershire sauce
¾ teaspoon minced fresh chives
Hot pepper sauce
Salt and freshly ground pepper

2½ pounds medium shrimp (or large shrimp cut into cracker-size pieces), cooked, shelled and deveined.

Combine all ingredients except shrimp in large salad bowl. Refrigerate several hours or overnight. Shortly before serving, add shrimp and toss thoroughly.

Crocked Shrimp and Cheese with Cucumber Rounds

This zesty spread also goes well with toast points and crackers.

10 servings

2 cups water
1 cup dry white wine
1 lemon, sliced
2 garlic cloves, peeled
1 teaspoon black peppercorns
1 teaspoon yellow mustard seed
1 pound uncooked unshelled medium shrimp

9 ounces cream cheese
3 anchovy fillets, rinsed

3 tablespoons butter, room temperature
1 tablespoon fresh lemon juice
1 to 2 teaspoons Dijon mustard
2 small green onions, minced
1 tablespoon capers, rinsed and drained
Salt and freshly ground pepper
2 cucumbers, cut into thin rounds

Combine water, wine, lemon, garlic, peppercorns and mustard seed in medium saucepan over high heat and bring to boil. Cover partially and let boil 10 minutes. Reduce heat to medium low, add shrimp and simmer 2 minutes. Set aside to cool. Chill shrimp in cooking liquid overnight.

Drain shrimp well; remove shells and devein. Combine cream cheese, anchovies, butter, lemon juice and mustard in processor or blender and mix until smooth. Add shrimp and chop finely using on/off turns. Transfer to medium bowl. Blend in green onion, capers, salt and pepper. Pack mixture into crock or bowl. Cover and refrigerate overnight. To serve, center crock on platter and surround with sliced cucumber.

Shrimp Butter Sauce

Serve with fish, shellfish, poached eggs or fresh pasta.

Makes about 1⅓ cups

Shrimp Stock
- 1 tablespoon vegetable oil
- 1 tablespoon butter
- ½ cup chopped onion (about ½ onion)
- ¾ pound uncooked unshelled medium shrimp
- 3 medium tomatoes, peeled, seeded, juiced and chopped (about 1¾ cups)
- ½ cup dry white wine
- ½ cup water
- 5 parsley sprigs
- 1 thyme sprig or ½ teaspoon dried, crumbled
- ½ bay leaf

- ⅓ cup dry white wine
- 2 tablespoons white wine vinegar
- 2 tablespoons very finely minced shallot
  Salt
  Ground red pepper

- 1 cup (2 sticks) well-chilled unsalted butter, cut into ½-inch pieces

- 1 teaspoon strained fresh lemon juice

For shrimp stock: Heat oil and 1 tablespoon butter in heavy large saucepan over low heat. Stir in onion, cover and cook until translucent, about 10 minutes. Add shrimp, increase heat to high and sauté until pink, about 2 minutes. Remove shrimp from pan using slotted spoon. Blend tomatoes into onion mixture. Stir in ½ cup wine, water, parsley, thyme and bay leaf and bring to boil. Reduce heat to low. Crush or chop half of shrimp and return to simmering stock. Shell remaining shrimp and reserve for garnish or another use. Crush or chop shells and add to stock. Simmer stock gently 40 minutes.

Combine ⅓ cup wine with vinegar and minced shallot in heavy-bottomed small saucepan over high heat and boil until reduced to about 2 tablespoons. Remove from heat. Strain shrimp stock into shallot mixture, pressing on ingredients with back of spoon to extract all liquid. Place over high heat and cook, stirring frequently and skimming occasionally, until mixture thickens and is reduced to about ⅓ cup, about 10 minutes. Blend in small pinch of salt and ground red pepper. *(Reduction can be prepared several hours ahead. Return mixture to simmer before continuing.)*

To whisk in butter: Remove saucepan from heat. Add 2 pieces of butter to reduction and whisk quickly until just incorporated. Place over low heat and whisk in remaining butter 1 piece at a time without stopping, adding each only after previous piece is just nearly incorporated; sauce should be thick and emulsified. (If at any time sauce becomes too hot and streaks or drops of melted butter appear, immediately remove sauce from heat and whisk in 2 pieces of butter. Continue whisking in butter 1 piece at a time, off heat, until sauce is thick and completely emulsified. Return sauce to low heat and continue whisking in butter 1 piece at a time.) Remove sauce from heat.

Whisk lemon juice into sauce. Adjust seasoning. Serve immediately. *(Sauce can be held for short period. Keep warm in vacuum bottle or on rack set above warm water; whisk often to prevent separating.)*

Shrimp with Rich Chive Sauce

4 first-course servings

Melted butter
Coarse salt
Freshly ground white pepper
24 uncooked medium shrimp (about ½ pound), shelled and deveined (reserve shells)

Sauce
Reserved shells from shrimp
1⅓ cups chicken stock
⅓ cup dry white wine
2 tablespoons chopped shallot
2 tablespoons chopped carrot
2 parsley sprigs
1 garlic clove, lightly crushed

1 cup whipping cream
1 tablespoon unsalted butter
1¼ teaspoons fresh lemon juice
½ teaspoon coarse salt
Freshly ground white pepper
Pinch of ground red pepper
2 tablespoons chopped fresh chives

Preheat oven to 450°F. Lightly brush 4 ovenproof plates with melted butter and sprinkle lightly with salt and white pepper. Arrange 6 shrimp pinwheel fashion on each plate. Sprinkle with salt and pepper. Press small piece of buttered waxed paper on top of shrimp. Set plates aside.

For sauce: Combine shrimp shells, chicken stock, wine, shallot, carrot, parsley and garlic in medium saucepan. Cook over medium-low heat until liquid is reduced to about ¾ cup.

Heat cream in small saucepan.

Transfer shrimp shell mixture to processor and mix 30 seconds. Sieve through fine strainer into another pan, pressing to extract as much liquid as possible from shells and vegetables. Set pan over medium heat and slowly stir in heated cream. Bring to boil, reduce heat and simmer slowly until sauce is thickened and reduced to about 1 cup. Remove from heat and beat in butter. Season with lemon juice, salt, white and red pepper. Stir in chives.

Bake shrimp 4 minutes. Remove plates from oven, discard waxed paper and let plates stand for 40 seconds. Pour about 2 tablespoons sauce over each portion and serve immediately.

Chutney Shrimp on Shells of Pastry

6 servings

1 recipe single 10-inch pie crust
6 4- to 5-inch extra-deep scallop shells
½ cup chopped onion
¼ cup (½ stick) butter
2½ teaspoons curry powder or to taste

½ cup chopped chutney (mango preferred)
3 cups cooked small shrimp, shelled and deveined
1 finely chopped hard-cooked egg
3 tablespoons minced parsley

For pastry shells: Preheat oven to 375°F. Prepare pie crust and roll pastry ⅛ inch thick on lightly floured surface. Oil each scallop shell and line with pastry, trimming edges with dull knife. Gently press pastry against shell so all indentations will be imprinted in the pastry. Place parchment or heavy duty waxed paper atop pastry and weight down with one layer of baker's aluminum pellets,* dried lima beans or rice. Bake on middle rack about 10 minutes, or until pastry shells are golden. Allow to cool before removing pastry from shell.

Baked shells may be frozen for 2 weeks. Be very careful when wrapping. Bring to room temperature and freshen in 200°F oven 10 minutes before filling.

Pastry shells may also be baked in individual tart or cupcake pans.

For chutney shrimp: Sauté onion in butter until golden. Stir in curry powder and chutney; mix well. Add shrimp, tossing until well coated with sauce and heated through. Do not allow to boil. Spoon evenly onto pastry shells. Sprinkle with egg and parsley.

Chutney Shrimp is also delicious on rice or toast rounds.

*Aluminum pellets can be found at some department store houseware sections or gourmet shops.

Shrimp Mousse with Sauce Nantua

Nantua, a town in the French-Comté, celebrates its catch of crayfish with a suave béchamel and shellfish butter that enriches any seafood. A lighter velouté base is used in this version to underscore the gossamer shrimp mousse. Preparation order is flexible, but it is usually most convenient to put the shellfish butter and stock together early in the morning and delay making the sauce until an hour before serving. The mousse can be assembled anytime and refrigerated, but it should not be baked until it is to be served.

4 first-course servings

1½ pounds uncooked unshelled medium shrimp (¾ pound shrimp meat)

Shrimp Stock
3 tablespoons butter
1 small onion, sliced
1 celery stalk, sliced
1 medium carrot, sliced
1 bay leaf
1 sprig fresh thyme or 1 teaspoon dried, crumbled
Several parsley sprigs
2 cups dry white wine or vermouth
1 cup water
¼ cup vinegar

3 tablespoons butter, melted

Shrimp Mousse
3 egg whites
1 cup whipping cream
1 tablespoon fresh lemon juice
1 tablespoon minced fresh dill or 1 teaspoon dried dillweed, crumbled
1 teaspoon salt
Pinch of ground red pepper

Sauce Nantua
2 tablespoons (¼ stick) butter
2 tablespoons flour
½ cup whipping cream
1 tablespoon fresh lemon juice
1 teaspoon salt
Pinch of ground red pepper

Shell and devein shrimp, reserving shells. Wrap and refrigerate meat.

For stock: Melt butter in heavy saucepan over low heat. Add shrimp shells, onion, celery, carrot, bay leaf, thyme and parsley and cook 30 minutes, stirring occasionally. Remove ¼ cup of shells and set aside. Add wine, water and vinegar to pan and bring to boil over medium-high heat. Reduce heat and simmer until reduced to 1 cup, about 1 hour. Strain, pressing to extract all juices. Set aside.

For butter: Combine reserved shrimp shells with 3 tablespoons melted butter in processor or blender and mix to a smooth paste, stopping to scrape down sides of container as necessary. Press through a strainer and refrigerate.

For mousse: Generously butter four 1-cup molds and line with buttered waxed paper. Wash shrimp if necessary and dry thoroughly with paper towels. Reserve 4 shrimp for garnish. Finely mince remaining shrimp with egg whites in processor or blender. With machine running, slowly add cream a drop at a time and continue mixing until pureed, stopping to scrape down sides of container as necessary. Season with lemon juice, dill, salt and red pepper. Place in molds and refrigerate.

For Sauce Nantua: Curl up the 4 reserved shrimp and secure with toothpicks. Melt butter in heavy saucepan over low heat. Add shrimp and cook about 1 minute on each side until they turn pink. Discard toothpicks and set shrimp aside until serving time.

Whisk flour into saucepan and let foam over low heat 3 minutes without coloring, stirring constantly. Whisk in cream and shrimp stock and stir over medium-high heat until sauce comes to boil. Reduce heat and simmer, stirring occasionally, until reduced by ⅓, about 20 minutes. Season with lemon juice, salt and red pepper. Keep warm.

To assemble: Preheat oven to 325°F. Place molds in baking dish and add water to come ¾ up sides of molds. Bring water to simmer over direct heat. Lay sheet of buttered waxed paper across tops of molds. Bake until mousse has puffed and drawn away from sides of molds and knife inserted in center comes out clean, about 20 minutes. *(If not serving immediately, turn off oven and let molds stand with door ajar.)*

Remove from water bath and let stand 5 minutes. Cut shrimp butter into small pieces and whisk into sauce. Run knife around edge of each mold. Drain any accumulated juices into sauce and blend well. Unmold mousse onto heated individual plates. Nap with sauce and garnish with reserved sautéed shrimp. Serve mousse immediately.

For lighter mousse with finer texture, strain mixture into bowl after adding egg whites. Set in ice-filled bowl and stir in cream.

Shrimp and Carnation Salad

4 servings

1 pound cooked shrimp, chilled
1 11-ounce can mandarin orange sections, drained
¼ cup thinly sliced red onion or ¼ cup chopped green onion
¼ cup almonds, lightly toasted
3 tablespoons fresh lemon juice
2 tablespoons honey
1 teaspoon sesame seed, lightly toasted
1 teaspoon salt
½ teaspoon ginger
Endive and watercress

4 carnations, washed (stalks removed and discarded) (garnish)

Combine all ingredients except carnations in large salad bowl and toss gently but thoroughly to mix. Divide among plates and garnish each with carnation.

Peasant Shrimp

A simple salad, white wine and French bread can accompany this easy supper.

4 servings

1 cup chopped fresh parsley
6 to 8 sprigs fresh tarragon or 1 tablespoon dried
4 garlic cloves, crushed
2 to 3 bunches green onions, thinly sliced
Juice of 3 lemons
½ cup (1 stick) butter
½ cup oil
24 uncooked jumbo or large shrimp, shelled and deveined (tails left on)

Coarse salt and freshly ground pepper

Combine parsley, tarragon, garlic, onion and lemon juice in medium bowl. Melt butter with oil in large saucepan over medium heat. Add parsley mixture and cook briefly until softened. Return to bowl, add shrimp and toss lightly. Cover and marinate at room temperature 1 to 2 hours, stirring several times.

Preheat broiler. Sprinkle shrimp with salt and pepper and toss lightly. Broil just until pink, turning once. Serve in soup bowls. Accompany with remaining marinade as sauce.

Shrimp Salad (Ensalada de Camarón)

Serve this appetizer salad mounded in a crisp tortilla cup or arranged on a few bright green lettuce leaves.

2 servings

2 teaspoons fresh lemon juice
¼ cup olive oil
  Salt and freshly ground pepper
1 cup cooked shelled shrimp, coarsely chopped
2 tablespoons minced white onion
1 small tomato, peeled, seeded and cubed, or 4 cherry tomatoes, halved or quartered

½ small avocado, peeled, seeded and cubed
2 teaspoons finely chopped fresh parsley
  Tortilla cups* or lettuce leaves

Place lemon juice in small bowl. Whisk in oil and season to taste with salt and pepper. Add shrimp and onion and toss lightly. Let stand about 15 minutes. Add tomato, avocado and chopped parsley and toss lightly. Mound into tortilla cups or on lettuce leaves.

*For tortilla cups: Press a corn tortilla into a large ladle. Holding it in place with a slightly smaller spoon, fry in deep fat (375°F) until tortilla is crisp. These can be held overnight in a turned-off oven. Tortilla cups are also pretty containers for guacamole or other dips and sauces.

Shrimp in Cucumber Nests with Dill Dressing

2 servings

1 large cucumber

8 cherry tomatoes

Dressing
1 egg
1 tablespoon fresh lemon juice
3 tablespoons olive oil
½ teaspoon dried dillweed

Salt and freshly ground pepper
½ bunch watercress
2 ounces cooked and peeled tiny shrimp

Peel cucumber, halve lengthwise and seed. Cut each half into 3 equal sections, then into thin julienne strips. Crisp in ice water for several hours.

Drop tomatoes into rapidly boiling water 10 seconds, then refresh in cold water. Peel and cut in half.

Whisk together egg and lemon juice. Begin adding olive oil slowly, beating until mixture is as thick as whipping cream. Blend in dill, salt and pepper.

When ready to serve, make bed of watercress on each salad plate. Top with cucumber arranged in nest. Mound shrimp on top and surround with cherry tomatoes. Dress lightly. (Refrigerate extra dressing for later use.)

Shrimp Fiji

6 to 8 servings

1 cup fresh orange juice
1 cup dry white wine
½ cup honey
1½ teaspoons grated fresh ginger

6 tablespoons clarified butter
12 garlic cloves, crushed

36 uncooked medium shrimp,
  shelled and deveined
1 tablespoon grated fresh ginger
1 cup slivered almonds
Freshly cooked rice

Combine orange juice, wine, honey and 1½ teaspoons ginger in small bowl. Set mixture aside.

Heat butter with garlic in wok or large skillet until butter is bubbly. Add shrimp and 1 tablespoon ginger and sauté briefly. Stir in almonds and continue cooking until almonds are golden and shrimp are cooked through. With slotted spoon, remove shrimp, garlic and almonds to heated platter. Pour off excess butter from skillet. Return skillet to burner and heat briefly. Add orange mixture and bring to boil. Reduce heat and simmer 1 minute. Return shrimp mixture to skillet and heat through. Serve immediately over rice.

Five Flavor Shrimp with Candied Walnuts

6 to 8 servings

2 quarts water
5 ounces walnut halves (1⅓ cups)
1 cup sugar
1 cup peanut oil

1 pound uncooked medium shrimp,
  shelled and deveined
  Pinch of salt
  Pinch of freshly ground white
  pepper
2 egg whites, lightly beaten
2 teaspoons sesame oil*
¼ cup (about) cornstarch

3 cups peanut oil
2 green bell peppers, seeded,
  deveined and cut into 1-inch
  triangles

4 ounces small snow peas, strings
  removed

2 green onions, chopped
3 garlic cloves, chopped
2 dried red chilies, chopped
1 slice fresh ginger, chopped
½ cup catsup
3 tablespoons soy sauce
3 tablespoons sugar
½ teaspoon salt
1 tablespoon sesame oil

Bring water to rapid boil in medium saucepan over high heat. Add walnuts and boil 7 minutes. Blend in 1 cup sugar and cook, stirring occasionally, until almost dry, about 1½ hours, reducing heat toward end of cooking time to prevent burning. Remove walnuts from heat and drain. Heat 1 cup peanut oil in wok or large skillet to 350°F. Add walnuts and fry 4 minutes. Remove and drain well on paper towels. Discard oil.

Sprinkle shrimp with salt and white pepper. Combine egg whites and sesame oil in large bowl and blend well. Add shrimp and stir to coat. Let stand 3 to 5 minutes. Dust with cornstarch, tossing until shrimp are well coated; shake off excess. Separate shrimp.

Heat 3 cups peanut oil in wok or large skillet over high heat until smoking. Add shrimp (in batches if necessary) and fry until crisp, about 3 minutes. Remove with slotted spoon and drain well on paper towels. Add green pepper and snow peas to oil and fry 30 seconds. Remove with slotted spoon and drain well.

Away from flame, pour off all but 2 tablespoons oil from wok. Add green onion, garlic, chilies and ginger and stir-fry 20 seconds. Stir in catsup, soy sauce, 3 tablespoons sugar and ½ teaspoon salt and bring to boil. Add shrimp, green pepper and snow peas and stir until coated with sauce, about 45 seconds. Blend in sesame oil. Spoon into heated serving dishes and sprinkle with candied walnuts.

*Available in oriental markets.

Grilled Shrimp

2 servings

½ cup dry breadcrumbs
⅓ cup olive oil
1 garlic clove, minced
1 tablespoon minced fresh parsley
1½ teaspoons finely chopped fresh basil

Salt and freshly ground pepper
1 pound uncooked large shrimp (15 or less), shelled and deveined

Combine first 5 ingredients with salt and pepper to taste. Pat generous amount onto each shrimp. Cover and refrigerate at least 2 hours, preferably overnight.

Position rack in upper third of oven and preheat to 425°F. Place shrimp on baking sheet and bake, turning once, until shrimp lose translucency and coating is golden brown, about 3 to 4 minutes per side (depending on size of shrimp).

Shrimp Grilled in a Wrapper of Seaweed

8 to 12 servings

24 uncooked large shrimp, shelled and deveined
2 tablespoons saké or dry Sherry
2 tablespoons soy sauce

4 sheets nori* (dried seaweed) or foil

Make small vertical slashes along underside of shrimp and straighten. Combine saké and soy sauce in large bowl. Add shrimp and allow to marinate for 1 hour at room temperature.

Prepare charcoal grill. Drain shrimp. Cut seaweed (or foil) into small pieces with scissors and wrap tightly around each shrimp. Arrange shrimp on grill seam side down. Grill until seaweed is glazed, about 10 to 15 minutes.

*Available in oriental grocery stores.

Baked Prawns with Garlic and Herbs

4 to 6 servings

½ cup olive oil
½ cup dry vermouth
⅓ cup fresh lemon juice
¼ cup finely minced fresh parsley
4 garlic cloves, finely minced
1½ teaspoons dried oregano, crumbled

Salt and freshly ground pepper
24 uncooked extra-large prawns, shelled and deveined (tails intact)

Combine first 6 ingredients in medium saucepan and bring to boil over medium-high heat, stirring frequently. Remove from heat. Taste and season with salt and pepper. Let cool. Arrange prawns in single layer in baking dish. Pour vermouth mixture over prawns. Let marinate at room temperature for 1 hour.

Preheat oven to 375°F. Bake prawns, basting once or twice, until pink and translucent, about 15 to 20 minutes. Serve hot.

Gingered Prawns

6 servings

1 tablespoon vegetable oil
2 teaspoons minced fresh ginger
12 uncooked large prawns, shelled and deveined (tails intact)

¼ cup light soy sauce
1 tablespoon finely minced garlic
1 tablespoon water
2 teaspoons sesame oil*

1 teaspoon white wine vinegar
1 teaspoon sugar

Chopped fresh cilantro (also known as coriander or Chinese parsley) or parsley (garnish)

Heat vegetable oil in wok or large skillet over medium-high heat until hot but not smoking. Add ginger and stir-fry 1 minute. Add prawns and stir-fry until just pink on both sides, about 3 to 5 minutes. Transfer to serving dish.

Combine soy sauce, garlic, water, sesame oil, vinegar and sugar in small bowl and blend well. Pour over prawns and toss gently. Cover with plastic wrap and refrigerate. Garnish with cilantro or fresh parsley. Bring prawns to room temperature before serving.

*Available in oriental markets.

Shrimp Etouffée

4 servings

½ cup (1 stick) butter
½ cup chili sauce
¼ cup chopped onion
¼ cup chopped celery
2 pounds uncooked shrimp, shelled, deveined and seasoned with salt, pepper and ground red pepper

¼ cup dry white wine
¼ cup chopped parsley
2 tablespoons minced shallot
Freshly cooked rice

Melt butter in large skillet over medium-high heat. Add chili sauce, onion and celery and sauté until vegetables are tender. Add shrimp and wine and sauté until shrimp loses its transparency, about 5 minutes. Stir in parsley and shallot. Serve immediately over rice.

Easy Scampi

4 servings

¾ cup (1½ sticks) unsalted butter
¼ cup finely chopped onion
3 to 4 garlic cloves, crushed
4 parsley sprigs, chopped
1 pound uncooked medium shrimp, shelled and deveined

¼ cup dry white wine
2 tablespoons fresh lemon juice
Salt and freshly ground pepper

Melt butter in medium skillet over low heat. Add onion, garlic and parsley and sauté until golden, about 10 minutes. Add shrimp and stir just until pink. Remove shrimp and place in ovenproof dish. Cover lightly and keep warm. Add wine and lemon juice to skillet and simmer about 2 to 3 minutes. Season to taste with salt and pepper and pour over shrimp.

Mediterranean Stir-Fry

2 servings

1 tablespoon olive oil
4 large garlic cloves, finely diced
2 red bell peppers, seeded and cut julienne
1 large onion, thinly sliced
3 cups broccoli (about 1 pound), cut into bite-size pieces and steamed until crisp-tender

2 tablespoons toasted unsalted pine nuts
1 tablespoon raisins
8 ounces cooked medium shrimp, shelled and deveined
Salt and freshly ground pepper

Heat oil in wok or large skillet over medium heat. Add garlic and cook, stirring constantly, until golden, about 1 minute (be careful not to burn). Remove garlic using slotted spoon and set aside. Increase heat to high. When oil is very hot, add pepper and onion and stir-fry until slightly softened, about 2 minutes. Mix in broccoli, nuts and raisins and stir-fry until broccoli is heated through, about 1 minute. Return garlic to wok with shrimp and stir-fry just until heated through. Season with salt and pepper. Serve immediately.

Simple Greek Shrimp

4 servings

¼ cup (½ stick) butter
1 large green bell pepper, seeded and chopped
1 large onion, chopped
1 28-ounce can stewed tomatoes
2 cups clam broth
1½ cups dry white wine

1 cup white or brown rice
1 pound medium-size shelled shrimp, cooked just until pink
2 6½-ounce cans minced clams, drained
1 cup feta cheese, crumbled

Melt butter in large skillet over low heat. Add green pepper and onion and sauté until crisp-tender, about 5 minutes. Add tomatoes, clam broth, wine and rice. Increase heat to medium high and boil 25 to 30 minutes. Add shrimp and clams. Reduce heat to medium and simmer 3 minutes. Transfer to serving dish and sprinkle with cheese.

Shrimp Connoisseur (Scampi alla Buongustaia)

This is a Roman specialty, traditionally served with golden brown Pan Dorato.

4 to 6 servings

1½ pounds uncooked large shrimp (about 15 per pound)
2 tablespoons flour
¼ teaspoon powdered sage
Freshly ground pepper
½ cup olive oil

¾ cup Sherry
1 tablespoon tomato paste

5 to 6 tablespoons water
Juice of ½ lemon
10 to 12 pitted black olives, sliced into rounds

1 tablespoon minced fresh parsley (garnish)
Pan Dorato (see following recipe)

Shell shrimp but do not remove tail. Wash and pat dry. Combine flour, sage and pepper in flat dish. Dredge shrimp in mixture. Heat oil in skillet (large enough to contain shrimp in one layer) over medium-high heat. Add shrimp and sauté on both sides *just* until they turn pink. Remove and keep warm.

Add Sherry to skillet, scraping bottom and sides to remove any clinging bits. Blend tomato paste and water, add to skillet and simmer 8 to 10 minutes. Return shrimp to skillet. Add lemon juice and olives and stir until warmed through. Turn into heated serving dish, sprinkle with parsley, surround with hot Pan Dorato.

Pan Dorato

6 slices white bread	Dash of allspice
2 eggs	
2 tablespoons milk or whipping cream	Oil for deep frying
Dash of freshly ground pepper	

Cut bread in half diagonally. Place in dish large enough to hold all slices in single layer. Beat eggs with milk or cream. Add pepper and allspice. Pour over bread, cover and chill 1 hour.

Heat oil to 375°F. Deep fry bread a few pieces at a time until golden brown. Drain on paper towels. Serve hot.

Shrimp Benihana

1 serving

4 to 5 uncooked large shrimp, shelled, deveined and flattened	Juice of ½ lemon
Salt	Benihana of Tokyo Ginger Sauce (see following recipes)
1 teaspoon butter	Benihana of Tokyo Magic
1 teaspoon whipping cream	Mustard Sauce (see following recipes)
2 tablespoons soybean oil	
1 tablespoon chopped fresh parsley	

Sprinkle shrimp with salt; set aside.

Combine butter and cream. Place griddle or large skillet over medium heat until hot. Oil griddle and add shrimp. Sauté until opaque, about 3 minutes on each side. Remove shrimp and dot with butter-cream mixture. Sprinkle with parsley and return to griddle. Cook 1 to 2 minutes longer. Squeeze lemon juice over shrimp and remove from griddle. Serve with ginger or mustard sauce.

Benihana of Tokyo Ginger Sauce

Makes about 1 cup

1 small onion, sliced	1 small piece fresh ginger or ⅛ teaspoon ground ginger
½ cup soy sauce	
¼ cup vinegar	

Place all ingredients in blender and mix at high speed for 2 minutes, until ginger and onion are finely chopped.

Benihana of Tokyo Magic Mustard Sauce

Makes about 1¼ cups

3 tablespoons dry mustard
2 tablespoons hot water
1 tablespoon sesame seed, toasted
¾ cup soy sauce

¼ garlic clove, crushed
3 tablespoons whipping cream, whipped

In small mixing bowl combine mustard and water to form a paste. Place in blender with remaining ingredients except cream and blend at high speed about 1 minute. Remove and stir in whipped cream.

Shrimp Jambalaya

8 servings

3 tablespoons vegetable oil
2 cups diced lean ham (about ¾ pound)
1 cup chopped onion
1 cup diced green bell pepper
1 cup chopped celery (including leaves)
3 pounds uncooked medium to large shrimp, shelled and deveined
1 1-pound can whole peeled tomatoes (preferably Italian style), drained and chopped (reserve juice)

2 cups water
1½ cups uncooked rice
½ cup minced fresh parsley
5 to 6 garlic cloves, sliced
1 to 2 small hot red peppers, chopped
1 bay leaf
1 teaspoon dried thyme, crumbled
1 teaspoon dried oregano, crumbled, *or* mixed Italian spices
1 teaspoon salt

Heat oil in large heavy saucepan over medium heat. Add diced ham and sauté just until cooked through but not browned, about 3 to 5 minutes. Stir in onion, green pepper and celery and continue cooking 1 minute. Add shrimp, chopped tomato and juice, water, rice, parsley, garlic, red pepper, bay leaf, thyme, oregano and salt. Increase heat to high and bring to boil. Reduce heat to medium, cover and simmer until rice is tender and liquid is absorbed, about 35 to 40 minutes; *do not stir.* Serve hot.

For spicier jambalaya, stir in ⅛ teaspoon filé powder or ¼ teaspoon hot pepper sauce at end of cooking time.

Sauté of Shrimp l'Antiboise

4 servings

8 to 10 Italian plum tomatoes, peeled, quartered and seeded
Salt

5 tablespoons full-bodied olive oil
1 medium zucchini, finely cubed
Salt and freshly ground pepper
1 red bell pepper, roasted, peeled, cored and finely sliced

1 small dried hot chili pepper, crumbled
1 pound uncooked shrimp, shelled and deveined

2 large garlic cloves, finely sliced
1 large sprig fresh thyme
3 tablespoons finely minced fresh parsley
2 garlic cloves, finely minced
2 tablespoons finely minced fresh thyme

Lemon wedges (garnish)

French bread

Place tomatoes in colander, sprinkle with salt and let drain 30 to 60 minutes.

Heat 2 tablespoons oil in heavy medium skillet over medium-high heat. Add zucchini, season with salt and pepper to taste and sauté until zucchini is nicely browned. Add red pepper and continue cooking for 1 minute. Remove from heat and set aside.

Heat remaining oil with chili pepper in heavy large skillet over high heat. When pepper has darkened, remove and discard. Add shrimp, sliced garlic and thyme sprig and sauté, shaking pan constantly, until shrimp turn bright pink. Season with salt and pepper. Discard garlic if it has burned. Add tomatoes and cook until excess liquid has evaporated, 2 to 3 minutes. Add zucchini mixture, parsley, minced garlic and thyme. Taste and adjust seasoning. Remove from heat and garnish with lemon wedges. Serve directly from skillet with French bread.

Shrimp Korma Curry

6 servings

6 tablespoons peanut oil
3 onions, cut vertically ⅛ inch thick
3 garlic cloves, minced
1 1-inch piece fresh ginger, grated
1½ cups water
1 bay leaf

1 teaspoon ground cumin
1 teaspoon ground coriander
1 teaspoon curry powder
½ teaspoon turmeric
½ teaspoon red pepper
Bouquet garni (2 whole cloves, 2 2-inch cinnamon sticks and 2 whole green cardamom pods)
3 tablespoons canned flaked coconut

½ cup buttermilk
½ cup canned coconut milk
1 cup plain yogurt
12 pitted dried apricots, chopped
3 tablespoons chutney, chopped
2 teaspoons coarse salt or 1 teaspoon regular salt
Freshly ground pepper

1 cup frozen peas, unthawed
3 tablespoons raw cashews
3 tablespoons canned flaked coconut
1 small onion, cut into ⅛-inch wedges
1 1-inch piece fresh ginger, shredded

2½ pounds uncooked jumbo shrimp, shelled and deveined
2 tablespoons fresh lime juice

Fresh cilantro (also known as coriander or Chinese parsley) *or* parsley
Garam Masala (see following recipes)
Rice (see following recipes)
Pappadams*

Heat 2 tablespoons oil in large saucepan. Add onions and cook about 3 minutes. Add garlic and ginger and cook 2 minutes. Add water and bay leaf; bring to a boil and cook until liquid is reduced by ⅔. Remove bay leaf from saucepan.

Heat 2 more tablespoons oil in a skillet over low heat. Add next 5 ingredients and bouquet garni and cook until spices release their aroma. Stir in coconut.

Add buttermilk, coconut milk, yogurt, apricots, chutney, salt and pepper to spices and cook 5 minutes, stirring occasionally. Remove from heat and discard bouquet garni. Combine skillet mixture with saucepan contents.

Drop frozen peas into boiling salted water for about 2 minutes. Drain; cool under running water and drain again.

For garnishes, heat remaining 2 tablespoons oil in a second skillet. Add cashews and stir until brown, about 3 minutes. Remove, then add coconut to skillet and cook over low heat until toasted, watching carefully. Remove. Add onion and ginger to skillet and stir-cook until crisp, about 5 minutes. Remove.

Add shrimp to same skillet. Add milk mixture and bring to a boil. *Immediately* reduce to a simmer, add peas and lime juice and simmer about 5 minutes; *do not boil*. Taste and adjust seasoning. Pour into serving casserole.

Sprinkle toasted garnishes around top. Place cilantro or parsley sprigs in center and sprinkle with Garam Masala. Serve with rice and pappadams.

*Pappadams are a dry, thin Indian bread available at specialty food shops. About 4 inches in diameter and packaged 12 to a box, they are available in three flavors: plain, mild, or hot with peppers (even the mild has some pepper).

To serve, heat oil in a 10-inch skillet to 360°F. Fry pappadams one at a time—they will inflate to twice their original size—until brown and crisp. Drain on paper towels.

Uncooked pappadams will keep indefinitely stored in a cool, dry place.

Garam Masala

Makes about 4 ounces

¼ cup cumin seed
¼ cup black peppercorns
¼ cup cardamom pods
2 tablespoons coriander seed
1 tablespoon whole cloves
1 tablespoon allspice
1 tablespoon fenugreek (optional)
3 2-inch cinnamon sticks

Preheat oven to 300°F. Put all spices on baking sheet and roast, stirring once, until they release their bouquet and are toasted, about 30 minutes.

Mash cardamom and peel off outside pod. Wrap cinnamon sticks in paper towels and mash with hammer or rolling pin. Combine all ingredients except cinnamon in blender and mix well. With motor running, drop in pieces of cinnamon and whirl until finely ground, scraping jar occasionally.

Transfer to strainer and sift onto sheet of foil. Return large pieces to blender and whirl again. Repeat until only hulls are left in strainer; discard hulls. Store in airtight jar in cool, dark place.

Rice

In Indian cooking the rice is served with a "self-garnish" of additional rice tinted yellow with turmeric.

1 teaspoon turmeric
Hot water
Cooked rice to serve 6

Measure turmeric into small dish, add about 2 tablespoons hot water and mix well. Pour over ¼ cup rice, toss and let stand 30 minutes. Drain, blot on paper towels and toss into remaining rice *just* before ready to serve.

Cheese and Shrimp Quiche with Mushrooms

6 servings

5 slices bacon
⅔ cup sliced mushrooms (about 4 large)
2 teaspoons finely chopped onion
1 unbaked 9-inch deep-dish pie shell
1 cup shredded Swiss cheese (about 3 ounces)
1 4½-ounce can small shrimp, drained
4 eggs, lightly beaten
1 7½-ounce can cream of mushroom with wine soup or 7½ ounces cream of mushroom soup and 2 tablespoons Sherry
¼ teaspoon freshly grated nutmeg
¼ teaspoon freshly ground pepper

Preheat oven to 350°F. Cook bacon in medium skillet over medium-high heat until crisp. Remove from skillet using slotted spoon; drain bacon on paper towels and set aside.

Discard all but 2 tablespoons drippings. Add mushrooms and onion to skillet and sauté until tender, about 4 minutes. Crumble bacon into pie shell. Sprinkle mushrooms, onion, cheese and shrimp evenly over bacon. Combine eggs, soup, nutmeg and pepper in medium bowl and beat well. Pour into pie shell. Bake until tester inserted in center comes out clean, about 35 to 40 minutes.

❧ Lobster

Lobster-Stuffed Cabbage with Chive Butter
(Le Chou Farci de Homard, Beurre de Ciboulette)

This is a specialty of Bernard's in Los Angeles.

4 servings

Court Bouillon
- 4 quarts water
- 1 750-ml bottle dry white wine
- 2 celery stalks, sliced
- 2 large onions, sliced
- 1 large carrot, sliced
- ¼ cup chopped parsley
- 3 cloves
- 6 peppercorns
- 2 teaspoons dried thyme, crumbled
- 2 teaspoons dried tarragon, crumbled
- 1 bay leaf
  Salt

- 2 1½-pound whole live Maine lobsters

Pike Mousseline
- 1 pound fresh pike, boned, or 1 pound fillet of sole
- 2 eggs
- 1½ cups whipping cream
  Salt and freshly ground white pepper

- 10 large savoy cabbage leaves, tough stems and veins removed

Chive Butter
- ½ cup whipping cream
- 1 cup snipped fresh chives
- 2 cups (4 sticks) butter, cut into tablespoon-size pieces

For court bouillon: Bring water to boil in 8-quart stockpot over medium-high heat. Add wine, celery, onion, carrot, parsley, cloves, peppercorns, thyme, tarragon, bay leaf and salt. Reduce heat and simmer 45 minutes.

Strain court bouillon and return liquid to stockpot. Taste and adjust seasoning. Place over high heat and bring to rapid boil. Gently drop in lobsters head first. Return to boil. Cook 5 minutes. Remove from heat and cool lobsters in court bouillon. Meanwhile, refrigerate processor work bowl (with Steel Knife intact) for at least 1 hour.

Drain lobsters; reserve court bouillon. Cut lobsters in half lengthwise; reserve any roe for mousseline. Crack claws and remove meat in 1 piece; set aside. Remove meat from body in 1 piece. Refrigerate until ready to use.

For mousseline: Place chilled work bowl and knife on base. Combine pike with any reserved roe in processor and mix to very fine paste. With machine running, add eggs through feed tube one at a time and blend until very smooth. Refrigerate mixture in bowl (with Steel Knife intact) at least 1 hour.

Return work bowl to base. With machine running, add cream through feed tube in slow steady stream and mix 1 minute. Season mousseline with salt and white pepper to taste. Refrigerate until ready to use.

To assemble: Blanch cabbage in large amount of salted water until just limp. Drain well; pat dry. Set 14 × 14-inch piece of plastic wrap on work surface. Arrange 2 cabbage leaves on plastic wrap, overlapping to cover any holes; use small pieces of another cabbage leaf to patch any particularly thin areas of cabbage (you will need 8 leaves total for recipe; the 2 extra leaves are for patching if necessary). Spread ¼ of mousseline evenly over cabbage. Arrange 1 piece of lobster body over mousseline, cutting lobster to fit if necessary (reserve any trimmings for garnish). Bring cabbage leaves up and over lobster, forming large sphere. Bring plastic up and over cabbage and twist top to seal and form tight package. Turn cabbage roll over (sealed end down) and gently press on all sides until symmetrical, then press top to flatten slightly. Repeat procedure with remaining cabbage, mousseline and lobster.

Lightly butter steamer rack. Position rack in steamer, large saucepan or stockpot. Add reserved court bouillon to within 1 inch of rack; do not let liquid touch rack. Place over high heat and bring to boil. Arrange wrapped cabbage rolls on steamer rack, spacing evenly; do not let rolls touch sides of steamer. Cover, reduce heat and steam gently 20 minutes. Add reserved lobster claw meat and continue steaming until cabbage rolls and lobster meat are heated through and mousseline is just firm, 5 to 10 minutes. *(Lobster claw meat may be finished before cabbage rolls; remove as soon as it is hot to prevent overcooking.)*

Meanwhile, prepare chive butter: Bring cream to boil in medium skillet. Stir in chives. Continue cooking until mixture is reduced by ⅓. Remove from heat and swirl in butter 1 tablespoon at a time until sauce is smooth and creamy. Season with salt and white pepper. Gently remove cabbage rolls from steamer; pat plastic wrap dry. Transfer rolls to individual plates. Carefully remove plastic wrap. Arrange smoothest side of roll up. Spoon sauce over top. Halve lobster claws horizontally. Set 2 claw halves cut side down in sauce on sides of roll. Garnish plates with any remaining lobster and serve immediately.

Haitian Lobster

4 servings

Sauce Caribe
¼ pound chopped fresh spinach
1¼ cups mayonnaise
3 anchovy fillets, finely chopped
2 small garlic cloves, minced
1½ teaspoons finely chopped chives
1 teaspoon finely chopped parsley
1 teaspoon capers
Juice of ¼ lemon
Salt and freshly ground pepper

Lobster
Oil
1 cup breadcrumbs
¼ cup ground almonds
1½ tablespoons chopped chives
8 4-ounce lobster tails, shells discarded
1 cup mayonnaise

For sauce: Combine all ingredients in small bowl and blend well. Cover and refrigerate overnight. (Let stand at room temperature about 1 hour before serving.)

For lobster: Heat oil in deep fryer to 350°F. Combine crumbs, almonds and chives in shallow bowl and mix well. Coat lobster with mayonnaise, wiping off excess. Roll lobster in crumb mixture, coating completely. Fry until golden brown on all sides, about 5 minutes. Drain well. Arrange on platter. Serve lobster with Sauce Caribe.

Crocked Shrimp and Cheese with Cucumber Rounds

Irwin Horowitz

*Pasta Primavera Salad with Seafood
and Basil Cream*

Dan Wolfe

Chutney Shrimp on Shells of Pastry

Brian Leatart

Mussels in Mustard Sauce

Brian Leatart

Peter J. Kaplan

Oysters Toscanini

*Marseilles-Style Grilled Skewers of Shrimp, Scallop
and Squid; Mediterranean Mussel Plaki*

From left: Halibut with Saké, Soy Sauce and Ginger; Tempura

Irwin Horowitz

Hot Sherried Lobster in Brioche

Fresh lump crabmeat or small cooked shrimp may be substituted for lobster.

4 servings

3 tablespoons oil
2½ cups cooked diced lobster
½ cup dry Sherry
3 tablespoons light soy sauce
1 tablespoon chopped fresh ginger or ¼ teaspoon ground

2 teaspoons cornstarch dissolved in a little water
¼ cup chopped green onion
4 to 8 brioches, hollowed, lids reserved

Heat oil in large skillet. Add lobster and Sherry and cook over medium-high heat 2 to 3 minutes. Lower heat to simmer. Add soy sauce and ginger and cook, stirring, 2 to 3 minutes. Add dissolved cornstarch and simmer another 2 to 3 minutes, stirring constantly, until sauce is clear and glazed. Add green onions. Place 1 or 2 brioches on each plate, fill with lobster, top with lid and serve at once.

Ragoût of Lobster with Morels
(Ragoût de Homard aux Morilles)

6 first-course servings

10 to 12 quarts (about) Court Bouillon (see recipe, page 75)
3 1½- to 1¾-pound whole live lobsters

Beurre Blanc
3 cups Fish Fumet (see recipe, page 72)
1½ cups dry white wine
½ cup mushroom stems or trimmings
2½ tablespoons Champagne vinegar
2 tablespoons minced shallot (about 1 large)
1 bay leaf
   Small pinch fresh thyme
4 cups whipping cream
2 tablespoons roux or thick velouté (optional)
½ cup (1 stick) chilled unsalted butter, cut into ¼-inch slices
   Salt and freshly ground white pepper

Lobster Sauce
2 tablespoons vegetable oil
¼ cup Cognac
2 medium onions, diced
2 medium carrots, diced
2 medium celery stalks, diced
2 teaspoons chopped fresh tarragon
2 bay leaves
   Pinch of chopped fresh thyme
1 pound plum tomatoes, peeled, seeded and chopped
3 cups dry white wine

⅓ cup dried morels (½ ounce)
2 teaspoons butter
1 teaspoon minced shallot
   Salt and freshly ground pepper

2 tablespoons (about) butter, melted
1 tablespoon (about) Cognac

6 tablespoons sliced leek, poached in chicken stock (garnish)
   Additional beurre blanc (optional garnish)

Bring enough court bouillon to cover lobsters to rapid boil in large stockpot. Add lobsters head first. Return court bouillon to boil. Cook lobsters until bright red and tender, about 10 minutes. Plunge lobsters into ice water; let stand 30 minutes to stop cooking process. Crack shells; do not cut meat. Cut through tail lengthwise. Holding lobsters over large bowl to catch juice, remove all shells, discarding head. Reserve meat, shells and juice.

For beurre blanc: Combine fish fumet, wine, mushrooms, vinegar, shallot, bay leaf and thyme in heavy large saucepan and bring to boil over high heat. Let boil until reduced to about ½ cup. Add cream and boil until reduced by half, whisking occasionally. Whisk in roux or velouté if desired. Remove from heat and whisk in 2 slices of butter. Place over very low heat and whisk in remaining butter 1 slice at a time. (If at any time sauce starts to break down, remove from heat and whisk in 2 slices of butter.) Strain sauce through fine sieve. Season with salt and white pepper. Set aside at room temperature.

For lobster sauce: Heat oil in large skillet over medium-high heat. Stir in reserved lobster shells. Pour Cognac into corner of skillet, heat briefly and ignite, shaking skillet gently until flames subside. Add onion, carrot, celery, tarragon, bay leaves and thyme and sauté 5 minutes. Stir in tomatoes, wine and reserved lobster juice and cook until liquid is reduced by about half, about 20 minutes. Strain mixture through fine sieve or chinois set over bowl, pressing firmly with back of spoon to extract all liquid. Transfer liquid to saucepan. Place over medium-low heat and cook until reduced to ½ to ¾ cup. Blend in beurre blanc. Set aside.

Combine morels in small bowl with just enough lukewarm water to cover. Let stand until water is clear, changing water about 5 times, about 1 hour total. Drain well; pat dry. Trim off tough ends of stems. Melt 2 teaspoons butter in small skillet over low heat. Add shallot and morels and cook until morels are lightly glazed, stirring occasionally, about 10 minutes. Season with salt and pepper. Set aside for garnish.

Preheat oven to 300°F to 325°F. Arrange lobster in shallow baking dish. Brush with melted butter. Sprinkle with about 1 tablespoon Cognac. Transfer to oven and heat through, about 3 to 4 minutes. Meanwhile, gently reheat sauce in top of double boiler over low heat, whisking constantly. Spoon lobster sauce onto heated individual plates. Arrange lobster decoratively on sides of plates. Garnish each serving with morels and leek. Fill 2 plastic squeeze bottles fitted with narrow tips with additional beurre blanc if desired. Pipe sauce onto plates in decorative pattern. Serve ragoût immediately.

❧ Mixed Crustaceans

Ramekins Fruits de Mer

6 servings

4 tablespoons (½ stick) butter
1 shallot, chopped
½ cup sliced mushrooms
½ teaspoon tarragon vinegar
¼ cup sour cream, room
   temperature
¼ teaspoon dry mustard
   Salt
1 cup coarsely shredded lump
   crabmeat

½ cup coarsely chopped cooked
   shrimp
1 egg, beaten
   Grated Parmesan cheese
   Italian seasoned breadcrumbs
   Paprika

Melt 2½ tablespoons butter in 10-inch skillet over medium-high heat. Add shallot and sauté lightly. Stir in mushrooms and vinegar and cook 1 to 2 minutes. Remove from heat and stir in sour cream, mustard, and salt to taste. Fold in crabmeat, shrimp and egg. Spoon into individual ramekins and sprinkle with Parmesan, breadcrumbs and paprika. Dot with remaining butter. Run ramekins under broiler just until golden.

Seafood in Phyllo

4 first-course servings

½ cup (1 stick) butter, melted and cooled
4 phyllo pastry sheets

Basil Sauce
1 tablespoon butter
2 teaspoons all purpose flour
¾ cup half and half
2 ounces cream cheese
¼ cup freshly grated Parmesan cheese
¼ cup dry Sherry

6 small fresh basil leaves or 1 tablespoon dried, crumbled
Freshly ground white pepper
Freshly grated nutmeg
½ cup cooked bay shrimp
½ cup crabmeat
⅓ cup freshly grated Parmesan cheese

Preheat oven to 375°F. Brush some of butter over 1 sheet of phyllo. Fold in half crosswise, brush with butter and fold in half crosswise again. Repeat folding twice, brushing with butter after each turn. Transfer packet to individual shallow baking dish (preferably shell shaped). Repeat with remaining phyllo. Bake until golden, about 20 minutes. (Retain oven temperature at 375°F.)

For sauce: Melt 1 tablespoon butter in medium saucepan over low heat. Add flour and cook, stirring constantly until smooth, about 3 minutes. Add half and half, increase heat to medium high and bring to boil, stirring constantly. Add cream cheese, ¼ cup Parmesan cheese and Sherry, stirring well after each addition. Reduce heat to low, add basil, white pepper and nutmeg and mix well. Remove from heat and set aside. Combine shrimp and crabmeat in medium bowl. Fold in ⅓ cup sauce. Spoon seafood mixture evenly over phyllo. Pour remaining sauce over each. Sprinkle with remaining Parmesan cheese. Bake until sauce is bubbly, about 10 minutes.

Crab and Shrimp Piquant

4 servings

6 tablespoons olive oil
5 to 6 anchovy fillets, mashed
¼ cup Creole mustard*
2 tablespoons red wine vinegar
1 tablespoon sweet paprika
½ teaspoon salt
½ cup thinly sliced celery heart
¼ cup minced fresh parsley leaves
2 tablespoons finely chopped green onion
2 tablespoons snipped fresh chives (optional)

½ pound cooked shrimp, shelled and deveined
½ pound crabmeat

Lettuce leaves

Chopped fresh parsley (garnish)

Whisk olive oil, anchovy, mustard, vinegar, paprika and salt in large bowl until blended. Mix in celery, ¼ cup parsley leaves, green onion and chives. Add shrimp and crabmeat and toss to coat with sauce. Cover and marinate in refrigerator up to 2 hours. Let stand at room temperature for about 30 minutes before serving.

To serve, line individual plates with lettuce. Top with seafood mixture. Sprinkle with chopped fresh parsley.

*Available in specialty food stores.

Seafood Cream Curry

This quick and simple curry is a favorite if you don't have time to employ every spice in the cupboard.

2 servings

2 tablespoons (¼ stick) butter
1 small onion, chopped
1 garlic clove, minced
1 teaspoon minced fresh ginger
1½ tablespoons all purpose flour
1 tablespoon curry powder
½ teaspoon salt
1½ cups warm milk

½ cup whipping cream
¼ pound small shrimp, cooked and shelled
¼ pound crabmeat
Fresh lemon juice to taste
Cinnamon Rice (see following recipe)

Lemon or lime wedges (garnish)

Melt butter in heavy skillet over low heat. Add onion, garlic and ginger and cook 10 minutes. Combine flour, curry powder and salt. Add to skillet and cook, stirring constantly, 5 minutes. Increase heat to medium and gradually whisk in milk, stirring until smooth. Reduce heat to low, cover and simmer sauce for 20 minutes, stirring occasionally.

Strain mixture into medium saucepan, extracting as much liquid as possible. Just before serving, add cream, shrimp and crab to saucepan and stir to blend. Place over medium-low heat and warm through. Add lemon juice. Spoon curry over Cinnamon Rice, surround with lemon or lime wedges and serve.

Cinnamon Rice

All the vibrant flavors of Indian food are set against the simple backdrop of rice.

½ cup long-grain rice (preferably basmati*)

6 cups water
1 tablespoon fresh lemon juice

1½ teaspoons salt
1 3- to 4-inch cinnamon stick
½ bay leaf

3 cups water

Place rice in strainer and rinse under cold water until water runs clear.

Bring 6 cups water to boil in large pot. Add lemon juice, salt, cinnamon stick and bay leaf. Slowly sprinkle rice into pot (water should not stop boiling). Boil uncovered until rice is tender, about 10 to 12 minutes.

Meanwhile, bring 3 cups water to boil. Preheat oven to 150°F to 200°F. Transfer rice to metal colander and drain well, discarding cinnamon stick and bay leaf. Rinse with 3 cups boiling water and drain again. Set colander on large baking sheet and bake until rice is snowy white and grains are separate, about 15 minutes. Serve immediately.

* Available in Indian food stores.

2 ❦ Mollusks

═══════════════════════════════════════

Recipes using mollusks—clams, mussels, oysters, scallops and squid—evoke such diverse images as hearty New England and seafood dinners, romantic picnics at the beach, elegant French suppers and easygoing lunches beside a Mediterranean pier. This flavorful seafood brings an infinite number of exciting possibilities into the kitchen, with an appeal that is obviously shared among cooks around the world.

To satisfy hearty appetites, try wonderfully lusty dishes such as Geoduck Stew (page 32) with a hint of filé powder or Oyster Rarebit (page 41). On the other hand, there is also a selection of distinctive low-calorie fare that will perk up any diet—Cosmo's Steamed Clams (page 31) in an herbed tomato sauce, Grilled Oysters with Ginger-Lime Dressing (page 39) and Calamari Vinaigrette (page 54) to name but a few. The versatility of mollusks is emphasized in the wide range of other dishes: appetizers such as sophisticated Mussel Soufflés (page 34) and Sea Scallops Set on a Mousse of Zucchini (page 51) and country-style accompaniments like Oyster Dressing (page 40)—great with the holiday turkey.

Other entrées can be centerpieces of fabulous new menus for entertaining. Steamed Littleneck Clams in Black Bean Sauce (page 30) is unique fare for an oriental supper, while Mussels in Mustard Sauce (page 37) is great for a casual dinner for friends. Just add a salad, a loaf of crusty bread and a chilled bottle of dry white wine and you're all set. Oysters Toscanini (page 42) with prosciutto filling and Mornay Sauce or Braised Scallops in Champagne Sauce with Sliced Kiwi (page 52) are perfect when the mood is more elegant.

In selecting clams, mussels and oysters for purchase, be sure the shells are tightly closed or close as soon as you touch them. Also make certain they feel substantial or heavy when held in the hand. Watch preparation time carefully—mollusks will toughen if overcooked.

These are among the most delicate and delicious foods from the sea. Whether you are serving them beachside or fireside, the following recipes showcase mollusks at their best.

❧ Clams

Clams Gourmet

8 servings

1 pound Monterey Jack cheese, shredded
3 6½-ounce cans chopped clams, drained
2 tablespoons finely chopped parsley

2 tablespoons chopped chives
2 garlic cloves, finely minced
Dash of ground red pepper
Dash of freshly ground black pepper
8 slices pumpernickel

Combine cheese, clams, parsley, chives, garlic and pepper and mix until well blended. For each serving place bread slice in 4-ounce soufflé dish or au gratin pan. Divide clam mixture among dishes. Broil until golden brown and bubbly. Serve immediately.

Steamed Littleneck Clams in Black Bean Sauce

6 servings

1 tablespoon peanut oil
2 teaspoons minced fresh ginger
1 garlic clove, minced
1 dried hot red pepper, finely chopped
¼ cup fermented black beans,* well rinsed and lightly mashed
½ cup clam juice, reduced to ¼ cup

1 teaspoon dry Sherry
1 teaspoon soy sauce
½ teaspoon sesame oil*

36 littleneck clams, scrubbed

3 tablespoons finely chopped green onion (garnish)

Heat oil in small saucepan over medium-high heat. Add ginger, garlic and red pepper and sauté until lightly browned. Stir in black beans. Add reduced clam juice and bring to boil. Season with Sherry, soy sauce and sesame oil. Remove from heat; keep warm. *(Can be prepared ahead and reheated.)*

Place scrubbed clams in large pot. Add enough cold water to come halfway up clams. Cover, place over high heat and steam until shells open, about 5 minutes. Discard top shells. Drain clams thoroughly.

Arrange 6 clams on each serving plate. Stir sauce through several times and spoon over clams. Garnish with green onion.

*Available at oriental markets.

Stuffed Clams

Makes 4 dozen

24 whole large clams

1 cup (2 sticks) butter
1 large onion, diced
1 large green bell pepper, cored, seeded and diced
3 celery stalks, diced
2 medium carrots, shredded

1 large garlic clove, crushed
1 tablespoon dried oregano, crumbled
1 6-ounce box garlic-onion croutons

12 slices bacon, cut into 3-inch pieces

Wash clam shells thoroughly under running water. Pour water into vegetable steamer to depth of 2 inches. Place clams on rack. Cover and steam until shells open, about 5 minutes. Discard any that do not open. Carefully transfer clams to work surface, reserving any liquid; chop clams coarsely. Set aside. Separate shells and clean each half thoroughly. Let clam shells drain; pat dry.

Melt butter in heavy large skillet over medium-high heat. Add onion, green bell pepper, celery, carrot, garlic and oregano and sauté until vegetables are tender, stirring frequently, about 10 minutes. Remove vegetables from heat and stir in clams and croutons.

Preheat broiler. Pack 1 tablespoon clam mixture into each half shell. Top with bacon. Broil until bacon is crisp. Serve hot.

This recipe can be halved.

Cosmo's Steamed Clams

6 servings

2 tablespoons olive oil
2 teaspoons minced garlic
72 littleneck clams
5¾ cups clam juice
3 cups water
1 16-ounce can whole tomatoes, crushed
1 cup dry white wine

½ cup (1 stick) butter
2 teaspoons salt
2 teaspoons crushed red pepper
2 teaspoons dried oregano leaves, crushed
2 teaspoons dried basil leaves, crushed
2 teaspoons chopped fresh parsley

In stockpot or Dutch oven heat olive oil over medium heat until haze forms. Add garlic and sauté until golden. Remove from heat and add remaining ingredients. Cover and bring to boil, stirring occasionally, until clams open, about 5 minutes. Remove from heat and let stand 5 minutes. Serve in soup plates.

Clams Pavarotti

4 to 6 first-course servings

2 tablespoons (¼ stick) butter
2 tablespoons olive oil
½ cup chopped onion
2 celery heart stalks, chopped
2 small garlic cloves, chopped
6 cooked cherrystone clams, chopped (reserve shells)
2 uncooked large shrimp, shelled and chopped
1 tablespoon chopped fresh parsley
¼ teaspoon dried thyme, crumbled

1 bay leaf
4 ounces crabmeat
Salt and freshly ground white pepper
½ cup Béchamel Sauce (see following recipe)
5 tablespoons freshly grated Parmesan cheese
2 tablespoons fine dry breadcrumbs

Preheat oven to 400°F. Melt butter with olive oil in medium skillet over medium-low heat. Add onion, celery and garlic; cover and cook until soft, about 10 minutes, stirring occasionally. Stir in clams, shrimp, parsley, thyme and bay leaf and cook until shrimp turn pink. Add crabmeat, salt and pepper and cook 5 minutes. Blend in 2 tablespoons béchamel, 1 tablespoon Parmesan and breadcrumbs.

Divide mixture among reserved clam shells. Top with the remaining sauce, dividing evenly. Sprinkle with remaining cheese. Arrange clams in pan. Bake until top is lightly browned, about 8 to 10 minutes. Serve hot.

❦ *A Traditional Clambake*

Long before the Pilgrims stepped off the Mayflower, American Indians had their first clambake. Pits dug deep in the sand were lined with melon-size rocks, then topped with driftwood and set ablaze. As the rocks heated, Indians gathered food for the feast—soft shell clams, corn on the cob, sweet potatoes, white potatoes and lobsters. When hot, the rocks were completely covered with wet seaweed. Then came the clams, a little more seaweed, the vegetables, and still more seaweed before the lobsters. The entire creation was covered with a final layer of seaweed and buried in the New England sand. After an hour or so, the feasting began.

The now traditional clambake has changed very little since pre-Colonial days. Some folks have added other ingredients—chicken, flat ocean fish, sausages and onions. And there is lively debate as to whether the clams (which should be soaked in freshwater for a few hours before cooking) should be on the bottom layer to provide extra moisture and flavor during the steaming process or on top so they can be eaten as a first course.

If you're far from the sea shore and you don't want to dig a hole in your backyard, you can still enjoy an authentic clambake. You need only a few things: a large wash bin or well-scrubbed aluminum garbage can to cook the food in; seaweed (order it from your local fish market, or use corn husks soaked in saltwater instead); and for each person: 1 lobster, about a dozen clams, 1 or 2 ears of corn (silk and tough outer husks removed), 1 or 2 potatoes, and other foods to suit the tastes of your guests. Cover the bin with a lid or a heavy tarpaulin weighed down on all sides and cook over an open fire. It's done when the clams begin to open and the potatoes are cooked through. And remember to serve it with plenty of melted butter—a delight the Indians didn't know.

Béchamel Sauce

Makes ½ cup

2 tablespoons (¼ stick) butter
2 tablespoons all purpose flour
½ cup milk
Pinch of freshly grated nutmeg

Melt butter in small saucepan over low heat. Whisk in flour and stir 3 minutes. Whisk in milk. Increase heat to medium high and cook, stirring constantly, until thickened and smooth. Blend in nutmeg.

Geoduck Stew

8 servings

2 tablespoons vegetable oil
½ cup chopped onion
½ cup chopped celery
½ cup chopped green bell pepper
¼ pound cooked bacon, ground
6 ounces cooked country sausage, crumbled
1 10-ounce package frozen okra, slightly thawed
½ pound diced geoduck clams or

other chowder clams
½ pound cod fillets, diced
2 cups Fish Fumet (see recipe, page 72)
2 cups tomato sauce
2 cups chili sauce
1 tablespoon fresh lemon juice or to taste
1 teaspoon filé powder*
Salt

Heat oil in large stockpot over medium-high heat. Add onion, celery and green pepper and sauté until soft but not browned. Stir in bacon and sausage. Reduce heat to low and cook 5 minutes. Separate okra and add to pan, sautéing briefly. Add clams, cod, fumet, tomato sauce, chili sauce, lemon juice, filé powder and salt. Continue cooking over low heat until okra is tender and stew is heated through, about 20 minutes.

*Available in specialty food stores.

🍒 *Mussels*

Steamed Mussels with Basil and White Wine

4 servings

4 pounds mussels, scrubbed and debearded*	¼ cup dry white wine
3 tablespoons cornmeal	3 large garlic cloves, minced
1 cup Lean Fish Fumet (see following recipe) *or* water	1 tablespoon minced fresh basil or 1 teaspoon dried, crumbled

Place mussels in large bowl. Cover with cold water and sprinkle with cornmeal. Refrigerate overnight.

Combine fumet or water, wine, garlic and basil in 6- to 8-quart stockpot. Drain mussels well. Add to stockpot. Cover and cook over medium heat until shells begin to open, about 5 minutes. When shells have opened *(do not overcook)*, transfer to four heated soup bowls using slotted spoon (discard any that do not open). Pour cooking liquid into bowl through strainer lined with 3 layers of cheesecloth. Ladle over mussels and serve immediately.

*Six pounds of small fresh clams can be substituted for mussels.

Lean Fish Fumet

Makes about 6 cups

2 to 3 pounds lean fish trimmings (heads and tails of carp, cod, flounder, haddock, perch, pike, snapper, sole, swordfish or whiting)	2 garlic cloves, unpeeled
	1 large carrot, chopped
	1 bay leaf
	¼ teaspoon *each* whole coriander seed and black peppercorns
4 whole cardamom pods	¼ teaspoon *each* dried basil and marjoram, crumbled
3 whole cloves	1 cup dry white wine
2 medium unpeeled onions, chopped	Water

Combine all ingredients except wine and water in heavy 5- to 6-quart stockpot over medium heat. Cover and cook, stirring frequently, until fish trimmings exude juices, about 10 minutes. Add wine and enough water to cover by about 2 inches. Bring to simmer slowly over medium heat, skimming off foam as it rises to surface. Cover partially and simmer 45 minutes. Taste stock. If more intense flavor is desired, continue simmering. Let cool. Strain into storage container through colander lined with three layers of cheesecloth. Refrigerate until ready to use. *(Stock can be refrigerated 1 to 2 days or frozen up to 3 months.)*

Mussel Soufflés

2 servings

¾ pound mussels, scrubbed and debearded
¼ cup white wine
¼ cup dry vermouth
1 shallot, minced
1 parsley sprig
1 bay leaf

1 tablespoon butter

1 tablespoon all purpose flour
1 egg yolk
Salt and freshly ground pepper

2 egg whites, room temperature
Pinch of cream of tartar

2 parsley sprigs (garnish)

Rinse mussels in several changes of fresh water. Combine wine, vermouth, shallot, parsley and bay leaf in heavy large saucepan. Add mussels and bring to boil over high heat. Cover and steam until mussels open, about 5 to 10 minutes. Remove mussels and drain well, reserving cooking liquid (discard any unopened mussels). Set aside 2 for garnish. Discard shells from all but 2 reserved mussels. Strain cooking liquid; boil over high heat until reduced to ⅓ cup.

Melt butter in small saucepan over medium heat. Add flour and cook 2 to 3 minutes, stirring constantly; do not let mixture brown. Whisk in reduced mussel broth and simmer until thickened, stirring constantly. Remove from heat and whisk in yolk. Stir in mussels. Add salt and pepper. Cool.

Position rack in lower third of oven and preheat to 375°F. Butter two 1-cup soufflé dishes. Beat whites until foamy. Add cream of tartar and continue beating until stiff but not dry. Fold ¼ of whites into mussel mixture, then gently fold in remaining whites, being careful not to deflate. Divide mixture between prepared dishes. Bake until puffed and golden, about 15 to 20 minutes. Set on small plates and garnish each soufflé with parsley sprig and 1 reserved mussel in shell.

Mediterranean Mussel Plaki

Fresh mussels on the half shell, bathed in a delectable sauce that should be soaked up with crusty bread.

12 servings

2 to 3 pounds mussels, scrubbed and debearded (about 18 to 22 per pound)
6 cups water

¼ cup plus 2 tablespoons olive oil
2 large onions, diced
2 medium carrots, finely diced
4 large tomatoes, peeled, seeded and diced (about 4½ cups)
¼ cup finely minced fresh basil
¼ cup finely minced fresh Italian parsley

1 tablespoon minced garlic (about 3 cloves)
1 teaspoon sugar
1 teaspoon salt
Freshly ground pepper
1 cup dry white wine or vermouth

½ cup pine nuts
½ cup currants

Lemon wedges and Italian parsley (garnish)

Combine mussels and water in 6-quart saucepan and bring to boil over high heat. Cover and cook 5 minutes. Remove any opened mussels. Continue steaming remaining mussels until opened, about 5 more minutes; discard any that do not open. Discard empty half shell. Set mussels aside (still attached to other half shell).

Heat olive oil in large skillet over medium heat. Add onion and carrot and cook until softened and just beginning to color, stirring occasionally. Add tomatoes, basil, parsley, garlic, sugar, salt and pepper. Increase heat to high and bring to simmer. Let simmer 5 minutes to blend flavors. Add wine. Cover skillet partially, reduce heat and simmer until slightly thickened, 20 to 25 minutes.

Add pine nuts and currants. Continue simmering until currants are plump, about 5 minutes. Remove from heat. Add reserved mussels on half shell (shells add flavor to sauce). Set mixture aside until ready to serve.

Remove mussels from skillet; loosen from shell but keep mussels in shell. Transfer to bowl or platter. Spoon sauce over each. Garnish with lemon and parsley and serve. *(Can be prepared ahead and refrigerated. Let stand at room temperature 1 to 2 hours before serving.)*

Mussels with Garlic in Wine Broth

2 servings

2 to 3 dozen mussels
Flour or cornmeal

2 tablespoons (¼ stick) unsalted butter
2 medium leeks (white part only), chopped
3 garlic cloves, minced

¾ cup dry white wine
¼ teaspoon dried thyme
½ bay leaf

⅓ cup minced fresh parsley

Salt and freshly ground pepper

Discard any mussels with open or broken shells. Scrub remaining mussels with stiff brush. Cover mussels with water mixed with a small amount of flour or cornmeal, and soak overnight.

Rinse mussels under cold water; clip off exposed beards with scissors.

Melt butter in Dutch oven or heavy large skillet over medium heat. Add leeks and garlic and sauté just until golden. Add wine, thyme and bay leaf and boil 2 to 3 minutes to reduce liquid slightly and concentrate flavors.

Add mussels and parsley. Cover and boil over high heat, shaking pan frequently, until shells open, about 5 to 10 minutes. Discard any unopened shells.

Transfer mussels to large shallow soup plates. Strain broth. Taste and season with salt and pepper. Spoon over mussels and serve immediately.

Moules Marinière

6 servings

5 pounds mussels, scrubbed and debearded (about 100 mussels)
1 cup chopped fresh parsley, lightly packed
¾ cup dry white wine
6 tablespoons (¾ stick) unsalted butter
3 tablespoons minced shallot

1½ teaspoons salt
1½ teaspoons freshly ground pepper

½ cup fish velouté
6 tablespoons whipping cream

Chopped fresh parsley (garnish)

Combine first 7 ingredients in 5- to 6-quart Dutch oven. Cover and bring to boil, then simmer until mussels open, about 5 to 10 minutes, turning occasionally. Transfer with slotted spoon to serving platter and cool slightly. Discard top half of each shell. Cover mussels with foil and keep warm.

Cook pan juices over high heat until reduced by ¾. Lower heat and, stirring constantly, add velouté and cream. When heated through, pour over mussels. Garnish lightly with parsley and serve immediately.

Malabar Mussels

Serve with pita bread and sesame butter. Clams may be substituted for mussels. Recipe can be doubled or tripled.

2 servings

2 tablespoons (¼ stick) butter
1 medium onion, minced
2 large garlic cloves, minced
1 teaspoon Garam Masala (see following recipe)
1 mild or hot green chili (Anaheim, jalapeño or serrano), minced, or 1 to 3 tablespoons minced canned chilies

2 ripe small tomatoes, peeled, cored, seeded and chopped
⅔ cup water
2 pounds mussels, scrubbed and debearded (about 40 mussels)
2 tablespoons fresh lemon juice

Lemon wedges (garnish)

Heat butter in heavy 4- to 5-quart saucepan over medium-high heat. Add onion and cook until golden brown. Reduce heat to medium and add garlic, Garam Masala and chili. Cook until aromatic, about 3 minutes. Stir in tomatoes and cook 2 more minutes. Add water and mussels. Cover and steam for a few minutes *just* until mussels open; *do not overcook*. Discard any mussels that have not opened. Sprinkle mixture with lemon juice. Transfer mussels to two large soup bowls using slotted spoon. Pour sauce over, garnish with lemon wedges and serve.

Garam Masala

A blending of roasted and ground spices that gives sparkle to cream-based sauces. Garam Masala can be frozen up to six months.

Makes about ½ cup

1 tablespoon cumin seed
1 tablespoon coriander seed
8 whole cloves
2 teaspoons whole cardamom seed (preferably green)

1½ teaspoons peppercorns
4 dried red chilies* or ¼ cup pure ground chili
1 teaspoon ground turmeric

Preheat oven to 300°F. Spread cumin, coriander, cloves, cardamom and peppercorns in shallow pan and roast 5 minutes. Add chilies and roast 2 more minutes. Remove from heat. Seed and devein chilies, if desired. Transfer spices and chilies to processor or blender. Add turmeric and mix to powder. Transfer to jar or bag, seal tightly and freeze.

*California chilies are mild, New Mexico "string" pods are hotter, ancho (pasilla) chilies still hotter and pequin or tepin chilies very hot. Choose according to your taste.

Warm Mussel Salad with Saffron

A specialty of Céline Menneveau of La Rôtisserie du Chambertin in Gevery-Chambertin, France.

6 to 8 servings

3 tablespoons unsalted butter
1 large leek (white part only), minced
2 tablespoons minced shallot
1 cup dry white wine or dry vermouth
2 cups Fish Fumet (see recipe, page 72) or clam juice
45 mussels, scrubbed and debearded (about 2½ pounds)

⅛ to ¼ teaspoon saffron threads, crushed in mortar

3 tablespoons olive oil

1 tablespoon minced shallot
3 tablespoons whipping cream

1 to 2 heads butter lettuce
Salt and freshly ground pepper

1 large celery stalk, peeled and cut into ¼ × 2-inch julienne (garnish)
1 large tomato, peeled, seeded, juiced and diced (garnish)
Fresh chervil leaves (garnish)

Melt 3 tablespoons butter in heavy large saucepan over medium-low heat. Add leek and 2 tablespoons shallot. Cover and cook until leek is tender, about 15 minutes. Pour in wine, increase heat and bring to boil. Let boil until reduced to glaze (about 2 tablespoons). Add fumet, reduce heat to medium low and simmer 5 minutes. Stir in mussels (in batches if necessary). Increase heat to medium high, cover and cook 5 minutes, shaking pan occasionally. Remove opened mussels from pan using slotted spoon. Cover and cook remaining mussels up to 5 more minutes. Remove from pan using slotted spoon; discard any unopened mussels.

Discard mussel shells. Strain cooking liquid. Return strained liquid to pan. Place over high heat and reduce to ¼ cup. Remove from heat. Add ⅛ teaspoon crushed saffron threads and stir to dissolve. Taste and add remaining ⅛ teaspoon saffron if desired.

Heat 3 tablespoons olive oil in heavy medium saucepan over medium heat. Add 1 tablespoon shallot and stir until translucent, about 3 minutes. Add cream and saffron mixture and bring to simmer. Add mussels and reduce heat so liquid is barely moving. Cook 5 minutes, stirring occasionally; do not overcook or mussels will be tough.

Meanwhile, tear lettuce into large bowl. Season mussel mixture with salt and pepper. Pour mussel mixture over lettuce and toss gently. Arrange salad on individual plates. Garnish with celery, tomato and chervil and serve.

Mussels in Mustard Sauce

Serve these steamed mussels in wide, shallow bowls. Accompany with a salad of escarole and curly endive.

4 servings

3 tablespoons butter
3 shallots, chopped
2 leeks, cleaned and finely sliced (white part only)
6 cups dry vermouth
6 pounds mussels, scrubbed and debearded (about 120 mussels)
¼ cup (½ stick) butter, cut into pieces

¼ cup all purpose flour
1 cup whipping cream
3 egg yolks, beaten
¼ cup Moutarde au Citron (see following recipe)
Salt and freshly ground white pepper

Melt 3 tablespoons butter in large saucepan over medium-high heat. Add shallot and leek and sauté until limp. Pour in vermouth and bring to boil. Add mussels, cover and steam until shells open, about 5 to 10 minutes. Transfer mussels to tureen using slotted spoon; set aside and keep warm.

Strain mussel liquid through fine sieve set over bowl. Measure 2 cups and pour into saucepan. Place over high heat and cook until reduced by half. Remove from heat. Mix butter with flour until well blended. Return mussel liquid to high heat and gradually stir in butter mixture, blending thoroughly. Reduce heat to medium high, add cream and cook until thickened. Remove from heat. Whisk in egg yolks and mustard. Place over medium-low heat and stir until thick and creamy. Season sauce with salt and pepper.

To serve, divide mussels evenly among bowls. Pass sauce separately.

Moutarde au Citron

Makes about 1 cup

1 cup Dijon mustard
1 tablespoon fresh lemon juice

1 teaspoon honey
Grated peel of 1 lemon

Whisk all ingredients in medium bowl. Transfer to jar with tight-fitting lid. Store in cool, dark place.

Feuilletés of Mussels la Napoule

8 servings

4 pounds mussels, scrubbed and
  debearded (about 80 mussels)
1 cup dry white wine
¼ cup minced shallot
1 teaspoon dried thyme
1 bay leaf
  Large sprig of fresh parsley

2 egg yolks
1 teaspoon cornstarch mixed with
  1½ teaspoons water

12 tablespoons (1½ sticks) well-
  chilled unsalted butter
  Fresh lemon juice
  Salt and freshly ground white
  pepper

8 feuilletés (see following recipe)
2 10-ounce bags (about 1¼
  pounds) fresh spinach, freshly
  cooked, drained and chopped

Combine mussels, wine, shallot, thyme, bay leaf and parsley in large stockpot.
Cover and steam over medium heat until mussels open, 5 to 10 minutes. Remove
mussels from pot with slotted spoon, shell and set aside. Strain liquid through
double thickness of cheesecloth into heavy-bottomed 1-quart saucepan. Boil over
high heat until reduced to ½ cup, about 20 minutes.

Reduce heat, add yolks and cornstarch mixture and whisk constantly until
sauce is thick and heavily coats spoon. Whisk in butter 1 tablespoon at a time,
making sure each tablespoon is completely incorporated before adding the next.
Add lemon juice, salt and pepper. Taste and adjust seasoning.

Fill each feuilleté with 2 tablespoons spinach and top with 5 to 7 mussels.
Spoon sauce over mussels, cover with pastry top and serve immediately.

Classic Puff Pastry

*Makes about 2 pounds of
pastry or 1½ to 2 dozen
feuilletés*

3 cups all purpose flour
  Pinch of salt
6 tablespoons (¾ stick) well-chilled
  unsalted butter cut into small
  pieces

1 cup *ice-cold* water

1½ cups (3 sticks) unsalted butter

1 egg beaten with 1 teaspoon water

Advance preparation: Place rolling pin (preferably ball-bearing type) in freezer
until ready to prepare pastry.

Combine flour and salt in large bowl and blend well. Add 6 tablespoons
butter and incorporate into flour with your hands until mixture resembles cornflakes. Add ice water and mix well. Knead dough until it is just smooth. (If dough
is sticky, add a little more flour.) Wrap well in foil and chill for 15 minutes.

Meanwhile, knead remaining butter with your hands until it becomes a pli-
able ball. Set butter aside.

Lightly flour large work surface and the rolling pin. Roll chilled dough into
a large square ¼ inch thick. Place kneaded butter in center and fold sides of dough
over butter as if folding an envelope, enclosing butter completely. Flour the dough,
transfer to plastic bag and refrigerate 30 minutes.

Lightly flour work surface and rolling pin again. Set dough in front of you
so the line of the last fold is perpendicular to you and to the right of you. Roll
dough into 18 × 8-inch rectangle approximately ¼ inch thick; do not roll completely to edges or butter may escape. When rectangle is 18 inches long, roll across
entire surface of dough to flatten ends and achieve uniform thickness. Brush excess
flour from dough. Fold dough in thirds as if you were folding a business letter,
making sure that edges match up perfectly, or there will be no uniformity in rising
once the dough is baked. This completes the first "turn." Cover and refrigerate
dough 1 hour or freeze 30 minutes. Dough should be firm but not hard.

Repeat procedure 4 times for a total of 5 turns, refrigerating dough 1 hour or freezing 30 minutes between each turn. Following the fifth turn, wrap and refrigerate the dough for 2 hours.

Position rack in center of oven and preheat to 425°F. Hold baking sheet briefly under cold running water. Shake off excess, then rub hand over sheet to make sure remaining water is evenly distributed. Line sheet with parchment.

With fold opening toward you, cut off 1-inch strip of dough using tip of sharp knife or pizza cutter. Roll strip into 12 × 2-inch rectangle ⅛ to ¼ inch thick. To promote even rising, trim ¼ inch of dough from each end.* Cut strip vertically into equal thirds. Turn rectangles upside down and place 2 inches apart on baking sheet. Repeat with remaining dough. Freeze 15 minutes. Brush rectangles with egg wash, being careful egg does not drip down sides of feuilletés, or it will act as an adhesive and prevent pastry from rising evenly.

Bake until feuilletés are golden brown and have risen 3 to 3½ inches, about 20 to 25 minutes, watching carefully last several minutes to avoid burning on bottom. Cut each feuilleté in half horizontally and carefully remove any uncooked pastry from center.

*Never discard puff pastry trimmings. They can be used for making any puff pastry that expands horizontally instead of vertically, such as *palmiers*. To maintain layering, piece them together edge to edge as you would a jigsaw puzzle rather than gathering into a ball. Roll out into new sheet of puff pastry ready for later use.

❦ Oysters

Broiled Oysters

6 appetizer servings

½ cup (1 stick) butter
1 cup Italian seasoned breadcrumbs
2 tablespoons dry white wine
½ teaspoon dried oregano

1 garlic clove, pressed
12 oysters on the half shell
Paprika

Preheat broiler. Melt butter in small saucepan over medium-high heat. Stir in breadcrumbs, wine, oregano and garlic and mix well. Spread over oysters. Place on baking sheet and broil 5 minutes. Sprinkle with paprika and serve.

Grilled Oysters with Ginger Lime Dressing

8 to 12 servings

Ginger Lime Dressing
½ cup grated Japanese radish (daikon)
¾ cup fresh lime juice
¾ cup rice vinegar

2 tablespoons grated fresh ginger
2 tablespoons soy sauce

24 oysters, unshucked

Combine radish, lime juice, vinegar, ginger and soy sauce in medium serving bowl, blending well. Set aside.

Prepare charcoal grill. Arrange unshucked oysters on grill and cook until oysters open, about 5 to 10 minutes.

Transfer oysters to large platter. Serve with Ginger Lime Dressing for dipping.

Oyster Dressing

4 to 6 servings

½ cup (1 stick) butter
1 cup finely chopped onion
1 cup finely chopped celery
6 cups seasoned dry bread cubes or packaged stuffing mix
2 eggs, beaten
1 teaspoon poultry seasoning

Salt and freshly ground pepper
2 cups (1 pint) chopped raw oysters (liquor reserved)
½ cup milk (or more)

Turkey drippings

Preheat oven to 350°F. Generously butter 2-quart baking dish and set aside. Melt ½ cup butter in large saucepan over medium heat. Add onion and celery and sauté until tender, about 15 minutes. Remove from heat. Gently stir in seasoned bread cubes, blending well. Add eggs, poultry seasoning and salt and pepper. Mix in oysters, reserved liquid from oysters and ½ cup milk. Toss lightly, adding more milk if mixture is too dry.

Turn into prepared baking dish. Cover and bake, basting several times with turkey drippings, about 50 to 60 minutes (baste frequently during last 10 minutes to ensure crisp top). Serve immediately.

Curried Oysters in Puff Pastry (Feuilletés aux Huitres)

4 servings

2 pounds Classic Puff Pastry (see page 38), chilled
1 egg, beaten

Sauce
⅔ cup Fish Fumet (see recipe, page 72)
⅔ cup dry vermouth
1 teaspoon curry powder
2 cups (1 pint) whipping cream
Salt and freshly ground pepper

4 tablespoons (½ stick) butter

Oysters
2 tablespoons (¼ stick) butter
2 bunches sorrel leaves (ribs removed), chopped

24 shucked oysters, liquor reserved

Line baking sheets with parchment paper; butter paper. Roll 1 pound puff pastry out on lightly floured work surface to thickness of ¼ inch. Cut into twelve 3 × 2-inch rectangles and arrange on prepared baking sheet. Brush tops with beaten egg. Repeat with remaining pastry. Refrigerate.

Preheat oven to 425°F. Bake rectangles until puffed and golden, about 20 to 25 minutes, watching carefully to prevent burning bottoms.

For sauce: Combine fish fumet, vermouth and curry powder in medium saucepan over medium-high heat and cook until reduced to 2 tablespoons. Add whipping cream and continue cooking until reduced and thickened. Season to taste with salt and pepper. Add butter 1 tablespoon at a time, whisking vigorously until well blended. Set aside and keep warm.

For oysters: Melt 2 tablespoons butter in skillet over medium-high heat, add sorrel and sauté 1 minute. Set aside.

Combine oysters and liquor in large saucepan over medium heat and cook until just warmed through.

To serve, cut each feuilleté in half horizontally through center, making 2 layers. Carefully remove any uncooked pastry from center. Place 1 tablespoon sorrel in each bottom half. Divide oysters evenly over sorrel. Nap lightly with sauce. Cover with top.

Oysters in Cream

6 servings

6 thin slices bacon, diced (about 4 ounces
1 tablespoon butter (if necessary)
2 leeks (white part only), thinly sliced (about ⅔ cup)
36 fresh oysters, shucked, or 36 canned oysters, well drained

¼ cup (½ stick) unsalted butter
¼ cup all purpose flour
1 cup half and half

1 cup whipping cream
½ cup fresh oyster liquor, Fish Fumet (see recipe, page 72) or clam juice
Freshly grated nutmeg
Salt and freshly ground white pepper

Watercress sprigs, minced fresh chives, and paprika (optional garnish)

Cook bacon in large skillet over medium-low heat until fat begins to render, about 3 minutes (add butter if bacon is very lean). Increase heat to medium, add leeks and cook until softened and just beginning to color, about 4 minutes. Add oysters, increase heat to medium high and cook, tossing gently, until oysters are just heated through and edges begin to curl, 2 to 3 minutes. Cover partially; set aside.

Melt ¼ cup butter in medium saucepan over medium heat until foamy. Add flour and whisk 3 to 4 minutes. Add half and half, cream and oyster liquor and whisk constantly until smooth, about 1 minute. Increase heat and bring to gentle boil. Reduce heat and simmer 10 to 15 minutes, whisking constantly. Add oyster mixture to sauce using slotted spoon. Cook until just heated through, about 5 minutes. Taste and season with nutmeg, salt and pepper. Spoon evenly over toast. Garnish as desired. Serve immediately.

Oyster Rarebit

4 servings

4 tablespoons (½ stick) butter
1 teaspoon Worcestershire sauce
½ teaspoon salt
¼ teaspoon dry mustard
Dash of ground red pepper
1 pound sharp cheddar cheese, cut into ½-inch cubes
½ cup beer or ale
2 egg yolks

8 large oysters, shucked

Flour
1 egg
1 tablespoon whipping cream
Freshly made cracker crumbs (preferably from saltines)
2 tablespoons oil
Salt and freshly ground pepper

8 toasted English muffin halves, toasted French bread slices *or* thick tomato slices

Melt 2 tablespoons butter in top of double boiler or chafing dish over simmering water. Add Worcestershire, salt, mustard and red pepper and stir well to blend. Add cheese. *Make sure water does not boil or cheese will become tough; some initial stringiness may occur, but cheese will incorporate as it warms.* Allow most of cheese to melt, stirring frequently. Add ⅓ cup beer or ale and continue stirring until cheese is completely melted. Beat yolks with remaining beer and add slowly to cheese mixture, stirring until blended and thickened. Keep warm.

Dip oysters in flour. Beat egg with cream in small dish. Dip oysters in egg and then roll in crumbs. Heat remaining butter and oil in skillet. Add oysters and brown well on all sides. Season to taste with salt and pepper. Divide oysters evenly over bread or tomato slices. Top with rarebit and serve immediately.

Baked Oysters

6 to 8 servings

24 large oysters, shucked and drained
Oyster Sauce (see following recipe)
2 pounds fresh spinach, blanched, squeezed to remove as much moisture as possible and chopped

12 strips bacon, cooked until crisp, drained and crumbled
Freshly grated Parmesan cheese
Paprika

Preheat oven to 375°F. Grease 2-quart shallow baking dish (or use 6 to 8 individual ovenproof dishes). Place oysters in single layer and top with Oyster Sauce, then spinach and crumbled bacon. Sprinkle liberally with Parmesan, covering spinach completely. Dust lightly with paprika. Bake uncovered until cheese begins to brown and bubble, about 12 to 15 minutes.

Oyster Sauce

2 cups mayonnaise
¼ cup chili sauce
2 tablespoons Dijon mustard
½ teaspoon paprika

3 to 4 dashes hot pepper sauce
Fresh lemon juice
Salt and freshly ground pepper

Combine all ingredients, adding lemon juice, salt and pepper to taste.

Oysters Toscanini

8 to 10 servings

Filling
2½ ounces prosciutto
4 large mushrooms (about 2½ ounces total), trimmed
2 shallots (about 2½ ounces total)
1 green bell pepper (about 2½ ounces), seeded and cut into chunks

1½ tablespoons butter
1 garlic clove, finely minced
2 tablespoons dry white wine
1 tablespoon minced fresh parsley
3 dashes bottled browning sauce
½ teaspoon minced fresh chives
¼ teaspoon dried oregano, crumbled
2 dashes hot pepper sauce
Salt and freshly ground white pepper

Mornay Sauce
1 tablespoon butter
1 tablespoon all purpose flour

1¼ cups milk
Freshly grated nutmeg
Salt
Pinch of flour
2 egg yolks, beaten
1 tablespoon freshly grated Parmesan cheese

Oysters
16 oysters, shucked (liquor and shells reserved)
Salt
Dash of fresh lemon juice

Rock salt
Freshly grated Parmesan cheese
Melted butter

Minced fresh parsley

Lemon slices (garnish)

For filling: Mince first 4 ingredients in processor or blender. Melt butter in medium skillet over medium-high heat. Add mushroom mixture and remaining filling ingredients and sauté 1 to 2 minutes. Remove from heat and set aside.

For sauce: Melt butter in medium saucepan over medium heat. Remove from heat and add flour. Cook, stirring constantly, about 3 minutes. Gradually add milk. Cook 20 minutes. Blend in nutmeg and salt. Whisk pinch of flour into egg yolks, then add yolks to sauce with cheese. Reduce heat to low and cook, stirring constantly, until thickened. Taste and adjust seasoning. Remove from heat and keep sauce warm.

For oysters: Combine reserved oyster liquor with salt, lemon juice and 3 quarts water in large saucepan. Add oysters and bring to boil over high heat. Remove from heat and let oysters stand in liquid to cool.

Cover bottom of roasting pan with 1 inch of rock salt. Clean and dry reserved oyster shells. Add 1 tablespoon filling to each. Drain oysters well. Arrange one in each filled shell. Mask with 1 tablespoon Mornay Sauce. Sprinkle with Parmesan cheese and drizzle with melted butter.

Preheat broiler. Arrange oysters and broil just until heated through. Brush with more melted butter. Arrange 1 or 2 oysters on each plate and sprinkle with parsley. Serve immediately with lemon slices.

🍇 *Scallops*

Scallops with Grapefruit
(Coquilles St. Jacques au Pamplemousse)

6 first-course servings

2½ quarts (about) Court Bouillon (see recipe, page 75)
2 pounds sea scallops

1 cup mayonnaise (preferably homemade)
2 tablespoons anise liqueur
1 to 2 teaspoons chopped fresh parsley (to taste)
1 to 2 teaspoons chopped fresh tarragon (to taste)

1 teaspoon Dijon mustard
3 medium grapefruit, peeled and sectioned
Freshly grated carrot (about 2 medium)
24 cooked large artichoke leaves, spiny ends trimmed to points
6 large radishes, very thinly sliced

Parsley sprigs (garnish)
24 raspberries (garnish)

Bring court bouillon to boil in deep heavy-bottomed 12-inch skillet. Reduce heat to very low; do not let bouillon return to boil. Add scallops and poach gently until just tender, about 2 to 4 minutes, depending on size. Transfer scallops to large bowl using slotted spoon. Let cool.

Blend mayonnaise, liqueur, parsley, tarragon and mustard in small bowl. Cut each scallop through center into 2 or 3 rounds. Arrange in 4 evenly spaced mounds just inside rim of individual plates. Place 1 grapefruit segment between each mound of scallops. Spoon small mound of grated carrot in center of plates. Arrange 4 artichoke leaves pointed ends out over mounds of carrot, spacing evenly. Spoon dollop of dressing over carrot, anchoring ends of artichoke leaves. Arrange radish slices upright in dressing in circular fashion, bending each slice slightly to form flower petal design. Roll up 1 radish slice and place in center. Tuck parsley around scallops. Garnish each mound of scallops with 1 raspberry and serve immediately.

Bacon-Wrapped Scallops

Makes 21 appetizers

1 cup all purpose flour
1 tablespoon salt
1 tablespoon paprika
1 teaspoon freshly ground white pepper
1 teaspoon garlic powder

21 sea scallops
1 egg beaten with 1 cup milk
1 cup breadcrumbs
7 bacon strips, cut into thirds
Tartar sauce or cocktail sauce

Preheat oven to 400°F. Lightly grease 9- or 10-inch pie plate. Combine flour, salt, paprika, pepper and garlic powder in shallow dish. Roll scallops in seasoned flour, shaking off excess. Dip into egg mixture, then coat with breadcrumbs, covering completely. Wrap each scallop in bacon and secure with toothpick. Transfer to prepared dish. Bake until bacon is crisp and scallops are cooked through, about 20 to 25 minutes. Serve hot with tartar or cocktail sauce.

Scallop Timbales with Watercress Sauce

8 first-course or 4 main-course servings

2 green onions
2 celery stalks
1 carrot
½ teaspoon dried thyme leaves, crumbled
½ teaspoon dried tarragon leaves, crumbled

1 pound sea or bay scallops
2 tablespoons (¼ stick) unsalted butter
Salt and freshly ground white pepper
1 cup dry white wine

4 tablespoons (½ stick) unsalted butter
1¼ cups milk
½ cup fresh breadcrumbs (made from firm-textured white bread)
4 eggs, lightly beaten
Salt

1½ cups whipping cream
1 bunch watercress leaves, chopped

Cut onions, celery and carrot into 2-inch lengths, then into julienne. Transfer to saucepan and add water to cover. Sprinkle with thyme and tarragon. Bring to boil over medium-high heat. Reduce heat and simmer 4 minutes. Drain and refresh in cold water.

Place scallops in stainless steel vegetable steamer (or colander) and set into large saucepan. Dot scallops with 2 tablespoons butter and sprinkle lightly with salt and white pepper. Arrange vegetables over top. Add wine. Cover and bring to boil over high heat, then reduce heat and simmer 5 minutes.

Remove steamer and let vegetables and scallops cool slightly; set saucepan with liquid aside for sauces.

Preheat oven to 350°F. Butter eight ½-cup dariole molds or ovenproof cups using 2 tablespoons butter. Divide vegetables into 8 portions. Chop scallops in processor or by hand. Melt 2 tablespoons butter in medium saucepan over medium heat. Add milk and breadcrumbs and bring to simmer. Let simmer 5 minutes, stirring frequently. Add scallops, eggs and salt and blend well. Fill each mold about ⅔ full, then insert vegetables upright into center of each.

Cover each mold with round of buttered waxed paper and set into large pan. Add enough boiling water to come halfway up sides of molds. Bake until set, about 20 minutes. Remove molds from water and let stand 5 minutes. Discard waxed paper. Unmold timbales onto warm plates or serving platter by running tip of sharp thin knife around inside edge of mold. Keep warm.

Return saucepan used for steaming to high heat and boil liquid until slightly thickened. Reduce heat; stir in cream and watercress. Simmer 10 minutes or until sauce is desired consistency. Taste and season with salt and pepper. Spoon over timbales and serve.

Poached Scallops in Emerald Hollandaise

Serve as an appetizer with French bread.

4 servings

Emerald Hollandaise
  4 **egg yolks**
  2 **tablespoons whipping cream**
  1 **teaspoon Dijon mustard**
  1 **teaspoon white wine vinegar**
  1 **cup hot clarified butter**
  2 **cups packed fresh spinach, cooked, drained, squeezed dry and finely chopped**
  3 **tablespoons finely minced fresh parsley (preferably Italian)**
  3 **tablespoons finely minced fresh chives**

Salt and freshly ground white pepper
  2 **tablespoons cold water (optional)**
  1 **teaspoon fresh lemon juice (optional)**

  3 **cups Vegetable Stock (see following recipe)**
  1 **pound bay scallops**

Parsley sprigs (garnish)

For hollandaise: Combine first 4 ingredients in blender and mix at high speed 20 seconds. Reduce to medium speed and add butter drop by drop until mixture is very thick. Add spinach, parsley, chives, salt and pepper and continue blending until smooth. Transfer to heavy saucepan and set in pan of *warm* water or store covered in wide-neck vacuum bottle. If sauce seems too thick, beat in cold water; if it is not tangy enough, blend in lemon juice.

Heat stock in 2-quart saucepan over medium heat. Add scallops and simmer until opaque, about 2 to 4 minutes; *do not overcook or scallops will be tough.* Drain thoroughly. Transfer to mixing bowl and fold in hollandaise. Spoon into shells or dishes and garnish with parsley. Serve immediately.

Vegetable Stock

Makes 4 to 5 cups

  2 **celery stalks (with leaves), diced**
  1 **large carrot, cubed**
  1 **large onion, sliced**
  1 **large leek (including 2 inches of greens), coarsely sliced**
  4 **to 5 cups water**
  6 **whole black peppercorns**
  3 **to 4 sprigs fresh parsley (preferably Italian)**
  3 **large unpeeled garlic cloves, crushed**

  1 **bay leaf**
    Coarse salt

  4 **to 6 whole white peppercorns, lightly crushed**
  2 **tablespoons white wine vinegar**
  1 **tomato (optional)**
  1 **large sprig fresh tarragon (optional)**
  1 **large sprig fresh thyme (optional)**

Combine first 4 ingredients in large nonaluminum saucepan. Add water, black peppercorns, parsley, garlic, bay leaf and salt and bring to boil. Reduce heat, cover and simmer 25 minutes.

Add white peppercorns, vinegar and optional ingredients and simmer an additional 10 to 15 minutes. Let cool. Strain. Cover and store in refrigerator.

Stock can be refrigerated for up to 3 weeks. Bring to boil every few days to prevent souring.

Grilled Scallops with Rice Vinegar Sauce

6 servings

Rice Vinegar Sauce
- ½ cup rice vinegar
- 1 shallot, diced
- ½ fresh green chili, cut into thin rings
- ½ cucumber, peeled, seeded and diced

- 2 tablespoons chopped fresh cilantro leaves (also known as coriander or Chinese parsley)

- 2 pounds sea scallops
  Olive oil

For sauce: Combine vinegar, shallot, chili, cucumber and cilantro in jar with tight-fitting lid and shake well. Let stand for at least 2 hours.

Soak 6 bamboo skewers in water 15 minutes. Meanwhile, prepare indoor grill. Thread scallops onto skewers, spacing evenly. Lightly brush scallops with oil. Grill until just firm, about 1 minute. Transfer scallops to individual plates (remove skewers if desired). Spoon 2 to 3 tablespoons sauce over each serving.

Scallops can also be sautéed. Heat about 2 tablespoons olive oil in large skillet over medium-high heat. Pat scallops dry. Add to pan (in batches if necessary) and sauté until just firm, about 1 minute, stirring frequently for even cooking. Transfer scallops to individual plates. Reduce any pan juices until thick. Spoon juices evenly over scallops with several tablespoons of sauce.

Scallop Kebabs

8 appetizer servings or 3 to 4 main-course servings

- 12 strips thinly sliced bacon, partially cooked until light brown and cut into pieces same size as scallops
- 16 sea scallops, halved horizontally
- 16 small water chestnuts, halved horizontally
- 32 5- to 6-inch bamboo skewers

- ⅓ cup soy sauce
- 2 tablespoons rice wine vinegar
- 1½ tablespoons sugar
- 1 tablespoon Chinese rice wine or dry Sherry
- 1 garlic clove, minced
- 1 teaspoon minced fresh ginger

Alternate bacon between scallop and water chestnut slices on skewers. Arrange in shallow dish. Combine remaining ingredients in processor or blender and mix well. Pour over kebabs, cover and marinate in refrigerator for 2 to 3 hours, turning skewers frequently.

Prepare fire, allowing coals to burn down to moderate temperature. Set grill about 4 inches above coals.

Spread coals in single layer. Drain off marinade and pat kebabs dry with paper towels. Grill until scallops are barely firm, about 6 minutes per side.

Cold Bay Scallops

2 to 4 servings

- 1 cup water
- 1 cup dry white wine
- 1 bay leaf
- 1 large slice fresh lemon
- 6 peppercorns
- 1 pound bay or sea scallops

- 1 cup sour cream

- 1 cup mayonnaise
- 2 tablespoons fresh dill
- 1 tablespoon fresh lemon juice
- 1 teaspoon salt
- ¼ teaspoon crushed garlic
- ¼ teaspoon freshly ground pepper
  Lettuce leaves

Combine first 5 ingredients in medium saucepan and bring to boil. Reduce heat and simmer 5 minutes. Add scallops and continue cooking until scallops are opaque, about 2 to 3 minutes. Drain in colander and rinse under cold running water. Cool slightly, cover and chill.

Combine all remaining ingredients except lettuce and blend well. Cover and chill until ready to use. To serve, arrange scallops on lettuce-lined platter and spoon several dollops of sauce over top. Pass remaining sauce in separate dish.

Seafood Boudin with Watercress Mayonnaise

10 to 12 servings

1¼ pounds sea scallops, well chilled
1 medium shallot
1 egg
1 teaspoon salt
Pinch of freshly grated nutmeg
Pinch of ground red pepper
1 cup Fish Fumet (see recipe, page 72), boiled until reduced to 2 tablespoons
¾ cup whipping cream
1½ to 2 teaspoons fresh lemon juice
1½ to 2 teaspoons Cognac

2 small carrots, cut into thin julienne (garnish)
1 leek (white part only), cut into thin julienne (garnish)
2 tablespoons water
¼ teaspoon salt

Watercress Mayonnaise (see following recipe)

Refrigerate processor work bowl, cover and blade until well chilled. Puree scallops and shallot in processor until very smooth, stopping as necessary to scrape down sides of work bowl. Mix in egg, salt and seasonings. Pass mixture through fine strainer if smoother texture is desired. Blend in reduced fish fumet, cream, lemon juice and Cognac. Taste and adjust seasonings.

Butter two 24-inch lengths of plastic wrap. Place 1 piece of plastic on work surface with long side nearest you. Spoon half of scallop mixture in 9-inch-long cylinder lengthwise across center of plastic. Bring far side of plastic over scallop mixture, smoothing out any air bubbles, and tuck under. Lift near side of plastic up and over scallop mixture, forming compact sausage. Twist both ends closed; bring ends up and over top. Gently smooth sausage with hands. Repeat with remaining scallop mixture. Rewrap each sausage with second layer of plastic. Refrigerate sausages if necessary to firm.

Lower sausages into deep wide skillet of hot water. Weight with plate to keep sausages submerged. Bring slowly to gentle simmer, then simmer until firm, with liquid barely shaking, 15 to 20 minutes, turning sausages once. Remove from heat and let stand in water 5 to 10 minutes. Using 2 spatulas, carefully transfer sausages to paper towel-lined rack. Let cool, then chill. *Can be prepared up to 1 day ahead to this point.)*

For garnish, combine carrot, leek, water and salt in small saucepan. Cover, bring to simmer and steam just until crisp-tender, about 4 minutes. Drain vegetables, cover and chill.

Carefully unwrap sausages, discarding plastic. Slice sausages diagonally. Arrange on chilled platter. Garnish with carrot and leek julienne. Accompany with Watercress Mayonnaise.

Watercress Mayonnaise

Makes about 2 cups

3 egg yolks, room temperature
2 teaspoons fresh lemon juice
1 teaspoon salt
Freshly ground pepper
1⅔ cups oil (half olive and half vegetable)

⅔ cup whipping cream, whipped
1 cup chopped watercress leaves
½ cup chopped fresh parsley
1 tablespoon fresh lemon juice or to taste
Salt and ground red pepper

Combine yolks, 2 teaspoons lemon juice, 1 teaspoon salt and pepper in medium bowl and whisk or beat until yolks are lemon colored and slightly thickened. Whisk in oil 1 drop at a time. When about ⅓ of oil has been added, whisk in remainder in slow, steady stream. *(Can be prepared up to 2 days ahead, covered and refrigerated.)*

Fold whipped cream, watercress, parsley, 1 tablespoon lemon juice, salt and ground red pepper into mayonnaise. Cover and refrigerate 1 hour. Taste and adjust seasoning.

Scallops Sauté

6 to 8 servings

2 pounds bay or sea scallops
Flour
Oil

¾ cup (1½ sticks) butter
2 bunches green onions, chopped
1 white onion, chopped
2 pounds mushrooms, sliced

2 tablespoons minced shallot
2 tablespoons minced garlic
1 tablespoon salt
2 teaspoons freshly ground white pepper
Juice from 1 lemon
2 cups dry white wine

Dust scallops with flour. Heat oil in large skillet over medium-high heat. Add scallops in batches and cook until lightly browned, wiping pan clean after cooking each batch.

Melt butter in large sauté pan, add onions and cook until soft. Stir in mushrooms, shallot, garlic, salt and pepper and sauté until mushrooms are tender. Add scallops, lemon juice and wine. Simmer 4 minutes, shaking pan occasionally. Do not boil. Serve hot.

Baked Bay Scallops

4 servings

1 cup (2 sticks) butter, room temperature
1 cup fresh breadcrumbs
6 garlic cloves, crushed
2 tablespoons finely minced onion
½ cup chopped fresh parsley
2 ounces (¼ cup) white wine or Sherry

Juice of ½ lemon
Salt and freshly ground pepper

2 tablespoons vegetable oil
2 tablespoons diced onion
1½ pounds bay scallops
½ pound mushrooms, sliced

Mix together butter, breadcrumbs, garlic, minced onion, parsley, wine, lemon juice and salt and pepper. Form into roll and wrap with waxed paper. Chill garlic butter until firm, at least 1 hour.

Preheat oven to 450°F. Grease shallow baking dish or au gratin pan. Heat oil in large skillet over medium heat until haze forms. Add diced onion and sauté until soft but not browned. Add scallops and mushrooms and salt and pepper to taste and sauté briefly. Drain off liquid. Arrange scallop mixture in prepared dish. Slice garlic butter and arrange evenly over scallops. Bake until butter is hot and bubbly, about 5 to 10 minutes. Serve immediately.

Scallops can also be broiled. Place about 3 inches from heat and broil until bubbly, about 3 to 5 minutes.

Capesante

2 main-course or 4 appetizer servings

2 tablespoons (¼ stick) butter
1 pound bay scallops
10 mushroom caps
1 tablespoon freshly grated ginger
⅔ cup dry white wine

1 tablespoon fresh lemon juice
1 cup whipping cream
Salt and freshly ground pepper
1 tablespoon freshly grated Parmesan cheese

Preheat broiler. Melt butter in large flameproof skillet over medium-high heat. Add scallops, mushrooms and ginger and sauté for 2 minutes. Transfer scallops and mushrooms to platter and set aside. Add wine and lemon juice to skillet, scraping up any browned bits. Cook until liquid is reduced by half. Blend in cream and continue cooking until reduced by half. Return scallops and mushrooms to skillet with salt and pepper and cook until just heated through. Sprinkle with Parmesan. Transfer to broiler and broil until lightly browned. Serve hot.

Scallops with Tarragon Herb Sauce

2 servings

1 cup white wine
2 green onions, cut julienne
1 carrot, cut julienne
1 celery stalk, cut julienne
Salt and freshly ground pepper
Pinch of dried tarragon, crumbled

½ pound bay or sea scallops (halve, if large)

1 egg yolk
¼ to ½ teaspoon fresh lemon juice
¼ teaspoon Dijon mustard

Pour wine in steamer and bring to boil over medium-high heat. Set vegetables on steamer rack. Sprinkle with salt, pepper and tarragon. Reduce heat to low, cover and simmer 4 to 5 minutes. Add scallops and steam until opaque and firm, 5 minutes. Remove rack; keep vegetables and scallops warm.

Cook steaming liquid over medium-high heat until reduced to ⅓ cup. Transfer to double boiler. Whisking rapidly, add egg yolk, lemon juice and mustard. Place over gently simmering water and cook, whisking constantly, until sauce has thickened. Arrange scallops on individual plates and nap with sauce. Garnish with julienne vegetables.

Velouté de Coquilles St. Jacques et Artichauts

4 servings

24 bay scallops
Salt and freshly ground pepper
2 tablespoons (¼ stick) unsalted butter
3 tablespoons finely chopped shallot
2 medium artichoke hearts, cooked until tender, diced

⅓ cup dry white wine
1 tablespoon Cognac
2 cups Fish Fumet (see following recipe)
2 cups crème fraîche

Sprinkle scallops with salt and pepper. Melt butter in large saucepan over medium-low heat. Add shallot and sauté until tender, about 3 minutes; *do not let shallot brown*. Add scallops, artichoke heart and wine. Cook until scallops are just done, 1 to 2 minutes. Remove from heat. Transfer scallops and artichoke to another large saucepan using slotted spoon. Sprinkle with Cognac. Set mixture aside and keep warm.

Add fish fumet to cooking liquid. Place over high heat and boil, skimming foam from surface as necessary, until liquid is reduced to ½ cup, about 30 minutes. Blend in crème fraîche. Return to boil, then reduce heat to low and simmer 1 minute. Pour through fine strainer into scallop-artichoke mixture. Place over medium heat and warm just until heated through. Adjust seasoning; serve immediately.

Fish Fumet

Makes about 2 quarts

¼ cup (½ stick) unsalted butter
1½ pounds fish bones and trimmings, preferably from sole or other white, firm-fleshed fish
1 cup chopped onion
1 large leek (white part only), halved lengthwise

1 ounce parsley with stems (about ¾ cup)
1 bay leaf
3 to 4 peppercorns
1 cup dry white wine
2 quarts cold water

Melt butter in stockpot or Dutch oven over medium heat. Add fish bones and trimmings, onion, leek, parsley, bay leaf and peppercorns. Cook 5 minutes, stirring frequently. Stir in wine. Simmer 5 minutes. Add water. Bring to boil, skimming foam as it accumulates on surface. Reduce heat to medium low and simmer 20 minutes. Pour through fine cheesecloth-lined strainer into large bowl. Skim fat before using.

Fish fumet can be frozen.

Shanghai Velvet Sliced Scallops

Juicy scallops in sweet-tart sauce.

2 main-course servings; up to 6 servings with other dishes

Marinade
1 egg white, beaten
2 teaspoons cornstarch
1 teaspoon salt
½ teaspoon Shaohsing rice wine*
¼ teaspoon sugar

1 pound sea scallops, sliced into discs ³⁄₁₆ inch thick

2 teaspoons minced green onion (white part only)
¾ teaspoon minced fresh ginger
¼ teaspoon minced garlic

Sauce
2 tablespoons Shaohsing rice wine

2 tablespoons light soy sauce
1¼ teaspoons sugar
1 teaspoon Chinese red wine vinegar
1 teaspoon cider vinegar
3 or 4 drops sesame oil*
⅛ teaspoon freshly ground white pepper

3 cups oil

Shredded snow peas (optional garnish)

Combine ingredients for marinade in bowl. Add scallops and mix well. Let stand at room temperature 30 minutes.

Meanwhile, combine green onion, ginger and garlic. Combine ingredients for sauce in another bowl. Set aside.

Heat oil in wok to 280°F. Drain scallops and reserve 1 tablespoon juice. Add scallops to oil and cook just until surface turns opaque white. Remove, drain and transfer to bowl to collect juices.

Pour out oil in wok. Add 1 tablespoon juice from scallops to wok and heat over medium-high heat. Add green onion mixture and stir-fry 30 seconds. Add sauce ingredients and bring to boil.

Reduce heat to low, add scallops, spreading as evenly as possible, and simmer until heated through, about 1 minute; *do not overcook.* Taste and adjust seasoning if necessary so sauce is just slightly sweet. Transfer to colorful dish, garnish with shredded snow peas, if desired, and serve immediately.

*Available in oriental markets.

Scallops Set on a Mousse of Zucchini

4 first-course servings

10 large sea scallops (about 12 ounces)
Melted butter
Coarse salt
Freshly ground white pepper

Zucchini Mousse
2 quarts (8 cups) water
2 tablespoons coarse salt
1 pound zucchini, thinly sliced

4 tablespoons (½ stick) unsalted butter, room temperature, cut into pieces

¼ cup leeks cut into 2 × ¹⁄₁₆-inch julienne (garnish)
¼ cup carrots cut into 2 × ¹⁄₁₆-inch julienne (garnish)
¼ cup zucchini cut into 2 × ¹⁄₁₆-inch julienne (garnish)

2¼ teaspoons fresh lemon juice
1½ tablespoons water
¾ teaspoon coarse salt
Freshly ground white pepper

Cut scallops in half crosswise. Lightly brush 4 ovenproof plates with melted butter and sprinkle lightly with salt and pepper. Arrange 5 scallop slices in center of each plate. Sprinkle with salt and pepper. Press small piece of buttered waxed paper onto scallops.

For mousse: Bring water to boil in large saucepan with 2 tablespoons salt. Add sliced zucchini and cook uncovered 3 minutes. Drain immediately in colander and let stand 20 minutes, shaking zucchini to remove any excess moisture.

Transfer zucchini to processor or blender in batches and puree until smooth. Turn into nonaluminum saucepan and bring to boil over medium heat, stirring constantly. Remove from heat and whisk in butter one piece at a time until mousse is smooth and all butter is incorporated. Set over hot water to keep warm.

Preheat oven to 450°F.

For garnish, bring another saucepan of salted water to boil. Combine leek and carrot in strainer and lower into boiling water for 30 seconds. Add zucchini strips and continue cooking 30 seconds. Remove strainer and let drain on paper towel, retaining water at boil.

Bake scallops 4 minutes. Meanwhile, stir lemon juice, water, remaining ¾ teaspoon salt and white pepper into mousse. Lower vegetables back into boiling water for 10 seconds to reheat.

Remove plates from oven and discard waxed paper. Spoon about ⅓ cup mousse around each serving of scallops. Garnish with vegetable julienne.

Sautéed Scallops in Mustard Sauce

4 servings

½ cup dry white wine
½ cup clam juice
1 tablespoon Moutarde de Meaux
¼ cup whipping cream

1 pound bay or sea scallops
All purpose flour
2 tablespoons (¼ stick) butter
2 tablespoons peanut oil

Combine wine and clam juice in small saucepan over high heat and bring to boil. Stir in mustard. Add whipping cream and blend well. Return to boil, then reduce heat and simmer until sauce is reduced by ¼, about 15 minutes. Keep warm.

Coat scallops lightly with flour, shaking off excess. Heat butter and oil in large skillet over medium heat. Add scallops and brown lightly on all sides. Pour off excess oil. Stir in sauce. Heat until scallops are cooked through and sauce is consistency of whipping cream, about 5 to 10 minutes.

Scallops Vera Cruz

Serve in individual scallop shells for artful presentation. The sauce can be cooked one day ahead and refrigerated. Add scallops and reheat in a low oven.

25 servings

1 cup olive oil
4 cups chopped onion
2 cups chopped green bell pepper
5 large garlic cloves, finely minced
2 bay leaves
2 teaspoons paprika
2 teaspoons dried oregano leaves, crumbled
½ teaspoon dried thyme, crumbled
½ teaspoon ground red pepper or to taste

4 28-ounce cans diced tomatoes, drained
1 16-ounce can tomato sauce

7 pounds scallops (leave whole if small; slice in half if large)
1 cup sliced green olives
¼ cup chopped cilantro (also known as coriander or Chinese parsley)
Salt

Heat olive oil in stockpot or large Dutch oven over low heat. Add onion, green pepper and garlic and sauté until soft but not brown. Blend in bay leaves, paprika, oregano, thyme and red pepper. Add tomatoes and tomato sauce. Increase heat to medium and bring to boil. Reduce heat and simmer 10 minutes. *(Can be prepared 1 day ahead to this point.)*

Add scallops and continue cooking over low heat (or in low oven if reheating later) until scallops are just done. Stir in remaining ingredients. Adjust seasoning and transfer to serving dish.

Braised Scallops in Champagne Sauce with Sliced Kiwi (Coquilles St. Jacques en Sauce Champagne au Kiwi)

4 servings

2 tablespoons (¼ stick) unsalted butter
1 large shallot, chopped
1 cup brut Champagne or dry white wine
Salt and freshly ground white pepper
1½ pounds bay or sea scallops

3 cups whipping cream
¼ cup (½ stick) unsalted butter, cut into pieces

2 kiwi fruit, peeled, sliced ⅛ inch thick (garnish)

Heat 2 tablespoons butter in large skillet over medium heat. Add shallot and sauté lightly. Add Champagne or wine and simmer until reduced by half. Season with salt and white pepper. Add scallops, top with piece of buttered parchment or waxed paper and simmer gently until just cooked through, about 2 to 3 minutes. Remove scallops with slotted spoon and keep warm.

Increase heat and reduce juices to a glaze. Blend in cream and simmer until thickened and mixture lightly coats spoon, about 20 minutes. Whisk in remaining butter. Taste and adjust seasoning. Divide sauce among warmed dinner plates. Arrange scallops over sauce and top each with slice of kiwi.

Scallops Provençale with Pasta and Avocado

Scallops can be prepared 1 day ahead. Reheat gently before adding to pasta.

4 servings

3 tablespoons light olive oil
3 tablespoons unsalted butter
1 pound sea scallops, trimmed and quartered

8 shallots, minced
8 green onions, minced
2 large garlic cloves, minced
2 teaspoons dried basil or 2 tablespoons minced fresh basil
1 teaspoon dried tarragon or 2 tablespoons minced fresh tarragon
¼ teaspoon dried thyme or ¾ teaspoon minced fresh thyme
½ cup dry white wine

4 cups well-drained, crushed canned tomatoes or 10 large fresh tomatoes, peeled, seeded and chopped
½ cup whipping cream
2 teaspoons sugar or to taste
Salt and freshly ground pepper
1 pound freshly cooked linguine
1 large ripe avocado, peeled, seeded and chopped

Heat oil and butter in large nonaluminum skillet over medium heat. Add scallops and sauté until barely firm, about 2 minutes. Using slotted spoon, transfer scallops to mixing bowl.

Increase heat to medium high. Add shallot and onion and sauté until soft. Stir in garlic and herbs; cook 1 minute. Add wine and cook 2 minutes more.

Stir in tomatoes. Increase heat to high and boil briefly until sauce is thick. Stir in cream and sugar and cook another 20 seconds. Season with salt and pepper. Add to scallops, mixing gently. Toss with hot pasta and divide evenly among serving plates. Top with avocado.

Miramonte's Scallops à la Nage

4 servings

1 cup dry white wine
2 shallots, finely chopped
4 peppercorns
1 pound large bay or sea scallops, cut crosswise into ½-inch slices

Beurre Blanc
½ cup dry white wine
1 shallot, finely chopped (about 1 tablespoon)

¾ cup (1½ sticks) unsalted butter, cut into small pieces
Salt and freshly ground white pepper
Pinch of ground saffron

Saffron threads, soaked in ½ cup water and drained (garnish)
4 watercress sprigs (garnish)

Combine wine, shallot and peppercorns in medium skillet over medium-high heat. Add scallops and poach 1 to 2 minutes. Drain well. Divide among 4 heated plates and keep warm.

For beurre blanc: Combine wine and shallot in 2-quart saucepan and bring to boil over medium-high heat. Reduce heat, cover and simmer 1 to 2 minutes. Increase heat to high and gradually add butter, whisking constantly until mixture is thickened and smooth. Add salt, pepper and saffron.

Spoon beurre blanc over scallops. Garnish with saffron threads and watercress. Serve immediately.

Miscellaneous Mollusks

Conch Fritters with Hot Sauce

Makes about 2 dozen fritters

6 large conch (about 1¾ pounds total), cleaned, blanched and finely chopped (about 2 cups)
1 large green bell pepper, seeded and finely chopped
2 medium-size yellow onions, finely chopped
1½ cups all purpose flour
1 cup milk
1½ teaspoons baking powder
1 egg
1 teaspoon dried thyme, crumbled

½ to 1 teaspoon minced fresh parsley
Pinch of paprika
Pinch of ground red pepper
Pinch of dried red pepper flakes or to taste
Salt and freshly ground pepper

Bacon fat and corn oil
1 cup hot cocktail sauce
1 teaspoon prepared horseradish

Chopped fresh parsley (garnish)

Combine conch, bell pepper, onion, flour, milk, baking powder, egg, thyme, parsley, paprika, ground red pepper and red pepper flakes with salt and pepper in large bowl and blend well. Let stand for at least 30 minutes.

Add equal parts bacon fat and corn oil to depth of 2 inches in heavy large skillet and heat over medium-high heat (or use deep fryer). Drop conch mixture into skillet in batches by teaspoons and fry until dark brown. Remove fritters using slotted spoon and drain on paper towels. Transfer fritters to baking sheet and keep warm in low oven while frying remainder. Arrange fritters on serving platter. Combine cocktail sauce and horseradish in small bowl. Set bowl in center of platter. Sprinkle chopped parsley over fritters and serve immediately.

Calamari Vinaigrette

6 servings

2 cups water
½ cup dry white wine
¼ cup fresh lemon juice
3 tablespoons olive oil
1 small onion, sliced
1 celery stalk, chopped (about ⅓ cup)
1 garlic clove, minced
1 bay leaf
½ teaspoon fennel seed
½ teaspoon dried basil, crumbled

10 whole black peppercorns

1 pound cleaned squid, cut into ½-inch pieces

Minced fresh parsley, chopped red bell peppers, Greek olives and marinated artichoke hearts (garnish)

Combine water, wine, lemon juice, olive oil, onion, celery, garlic, bay leaf, fennel seed, basil and peppercorns in large saucepan over medium-high heat and bring to simmer. Reduce heat to low, cover and cook 25 minutes.

Bring mixture to boil. Add squid and blanch for 30 seconds. Transfer squid to bowl using slotted spoon. Strain cooking liquid through several layers of dampened cheesecloth. Return liquid to saucepan. Place over high heat and bring to boil. Cook until reduced to ½ cup. Remove dressing from heat and allow to cool to room temperature.

To serve, arrange squid on large platter. Spoon dressing over. Garnish with parsley, red peppers, Greek olives and marinated artichoke hearts.

Squid Salad with Green Ginger Sauce

2 servings

1¼ pounds squid
Boiling water

Green Ginger Sauce
¼ cup vegetable oil
3 to 4 tablespoons green onion, finely chopped
2 tablespoons dry Sherry
1 1-inch piece fresh ginger, peeled and cut into several pieces
Juice of 1 lemon
Salt

2 green bell peppers, seeded and finely shredded
1 cup bamboo shoots, finely shredded
1 small leek (white part only), finely shredded
1 medium carrot, finely shredded

Open and clean squid. Score diamond pattern on underside and cut into 1-inch pieces. Cook in boiling water until white and curled, about 1 minute; *do not overcook*. Drain well and let cool.

Combine all ingredients for sauce in processor or blender and mix until onion and ginger are finely minced.

Combine remaining ingredients in bowl and toss lightly. Arrange on platter. Toss squid in sauce and arrange over vegetables. Spoon any remaining sauce over top. Serve at room temperature.

Shellfish with Red Pepper Sauce

6 servings

2 cups dry white wine
¼ cup (½ stick) butter
¼ cup minced fresh parsley
¼ cup minced shallot
1 bay leaf
Salt and freshly ground pepper
30 mussels, scrubbed and debearded
1 pound whole bay scallops or quartered sea scallops

3 large red bell peppers, cored, seeded and cut into large pieces
1 tablespoon butter, room temperature

Parsley sprigs (garnish)

Combine wine, ¼ cup butter, parsley, shallot, bay leaf, salt and pepper in large saucepan and bring to boil over high heat. Let boil 2 minutes. Add mussels. Cover tightly and cook 3 minutes, shaking pot vigorously every 60 seconds. Remove opened mussels using slotted spoon. Continue cooking unopened mussels 2 to 3 minutes, shaking every 60 seconds. Discard any remaining unopened mussels.

Discard mussel shells. Line strainer with several layers of dampened cheese-cloth. Strain cooking liquid twice. Transfer to large saucepan and bring to gentle simmer over medium heat. Add scallops and poach just until opaque, about 1 minute. Remove scallops using slotted spoon. Increase heat and cook liquid until reduced to 1 cup.

Place red pepper in processor and puree 5 *full* minutes. Transfer to heavy medium saucepan. Place over lowest possible heat and cook, stirring frequently, until nearly dry, about 20 to 25 minutes. Return to processor and puree 2 minutes. Press puree through fine strainer. Reheat reserved cooking liquid. Stir in pepper puree and butter. Season generously with pepper.

Divide mussels and scallops evenly among individual plates. Spoon sauce over. Garnish with parsley and serve.

Brian Leatart

Fish Balls with Snow Peas and Asparagus

Clockwise from right:
Steamed Mussels with Basil and
White Wine, Oven-Poached
Sole with Vegetables, a salad of
scallops and cucumbers

Irwin Horowitz

Brian Leatart

Salmon in Basil Sauce

Green Tortelloni Stuffed with Trout

Brian Leatart

Jerry Friedman

*From left: Risotto con
Frutti di Mare, Mixed Antipasti,
Sea Bass at Our Pleasure*

Boudins de Fruits de Mer

3 ❦ Saltwater Fish

This group of fish covers a lot of territory—the oceans of the world to be exact. Sea bass and striped bass, cod, flounder, halibut, red snapper, sole, herring, monkfish, pompano, swordfish and tuna are among the most plentiful fish available to the American shopper. A bonus to this selection is that these types adapt deliciously to many techniques of cooking and to all sorts of sauces and garnishes.

The recipes in this chapter take full advantage of the versatility of these fish. For instance, grilling lends an irresistible nuance to Crackly Crusted Sea Bass with Herbs (page 58), but the fish receives the glamour treatment in Sea Bass at Our Pleasure (page 58) and an entirely different flavor from poaching. Other great main courses using poached fish include Halibut with Saké, Soy Sauce and Ginger (page 81) and Cold Poached Snapper with Avocado Sauce (page 60).

Sautéeing and stir-frying are other popular methods for preparing ocean fish and are ideal for healthful main courses in a hurry. Some delectable examples in this collection are Red Snapper Szechwan (page 64) accented with chili paste and green peppers and Swordfish Steak with Lemon and Capers (page 76). Pat the fish dry with paper towels and be sure the skillet is hot before cooking to completely seal in the natural juices.

Cooking fish *en papillote,* a French technique that is easy on the cook, is an impressive presentation for company. Individual portions of fish, an accompanying sauce and occasionally chopped or julienned vegetables are wrapped in parchment paper or foil and baked just before serving. In many instances, these packets can be assembled ahead and refrigerated until you are ready to cook them. Each guest receives their own "surprise package" which they unwrap at the table to reveal the tempting contents within. Papillote of Sea Bass with Tomato Fondue (page 59) and Sole Fillets with Mushrooms and Apples Steamed in Paper (page 69) are two excellent ways to experiment with this unique format.

From stir-frys to elegant *en croûte* creations, from Ceviche to Tapenade, ocean fish can provide an unlimited bounty of new ideas that add excitement to any menu.

🍎 Bass

Crackly Crusted Sea Bass with Herbs

4 servings

1 3- to 4-pound sea bass, butterflied (with or without head)
Coarse salt and freshly ground pepper
Olive oil

½ cup mixed minced fresh herbs (parsley, tarragon, chives or thyme)
1½ cups coarse dry breadcrumbs

Prepare charcoal grill. Sprinkle inside of fish with salt and pepper. Brush outside generously with oil. Press herbs firmly into all sides. Repeat with breadcrumbs and drizzle with additional oil.

Place fish in hinged grill and cook about 10 minutes on each side, turning when fish barely loses its translucency and crumbs are crusty and golden brown.

Sea Bass at Our Pleasure

A literal translation of the restaurant Costa Smeralda's name for braised whole fish. They also grill fish or shellfish over a slow wood fire. Both methods accent the qualities of superbly fresh seafoods.

4 servings

½ cup all purpose flour
1 3- to 3½-pound whole sea bass*

2 tablespoons olive oil
1 tablespoon vegetable oil
3 tablespoons minced Italian parsley
2 garlic cloves, halved

⅔ cup dry white wine
⅓ cup Fish Fumet (see recipe, page 72) or chicken stock
3 fresh plum tomatoes, peeled,

seeded and coarsely chopped (about 1 cup), or 3 canned Italian plum tomatoes, drained and seeded
14 mildly cured Italian or Greek black olives, pitted
½ teaspoon fresh oregano or ⅛ teaspoon dried, crumbled
½ teaspoon fresh rosemary or ⅛ teaspoon dried, crumbled
Salt and freshly ground pepper
2 teaspoons butter

Sprinkle flour over large piece of waxed paper. Roll fish in flour to coat evenly, shaking off excess. Heat oils in shallow large roasting pan over medium-high heat. Add fish and parsley and sear fish on both sides until very lightly golden, using wooden spatulas to turn fish carefully. Add garlic to pan. Set aside in cool place (do not refrigerate) for up to 45 minutes.

About 25 minutes before serving, preheat oven to 350°F. Place roasting pan over medium-high heat. Add wine, fumet, tomatoes, olives, oregano and rosemary to fish. Season with salt and pepper. Bring liquid to simmer. Transfer to oven and bake just until flesh at thickest part of fish is completely opaque to the bone, about 20 minutes (or 8 minutes per inch of thickness). Carefully transfer fish to serving platter. Discard garlic. Place pan over high heat and boil until liquid is thickened and reduced by about ⅓. Swirl in butter, blending well. Pour sauce around fish and serve immediately.

To cut fish into servings, run sharp knife about ½ inch in from backbone (to avoid any tiny bones). Repeat along other side. Cut fillet in half crosswise in center of fish. Using flat fish server, gently loosen fillet halves from bone, then transfer to plates. Remove skeleton. Cut bottom fillet in half crosswise. Cut away long row of tiny backbones. Transfer fillet to plates.

*Other firm-fleshed fish such as bluefish, rock bass, golden bass or sea trout can be used. Adjust baking times accordingly.

Papillote of Sea Bass with Tomato Fondue

4 servings

Tomato Fondue
- 3 tablespoons unsalted butter
- 2¼ pounds firm ripe tomatoes, peeled, seeded and cut into thin strips (about 5 large tomatoes)
- Salt and freshly ground pepper
- ½ teaspoon minced fresh tarragon leaves

  Melted butter
- 4 4-ounce sea bass fillets, about ¾ inch thick, or other firm-fleshed white fish fillets

Tomato Sauce
- ¼ cup plus 3 tablespoons dry white wine
- 3½ tablespoons white wine vinegar
- 2 tablespoons minced shallot
- 1½ teaspoons chopped preserved (in vinegar) tarragon leaves
- ½ cup plus 2 tablespoons (1¼ sticks) unsalted butter
- 4 egg yolks, room temperature
- 1 tablespoon cold water
- ½ teaspoon minced fresh tarragon leaves or more to taste

For fondue: Melt 3 tablespoons butter in large skillet over medium-low heat. Add tomatoes and cook until softened, about 5 minutes; do not break up tomatoes. Season with salt and pepper. Gently blend in ½ teaspoon minced fresh tarragon leaves. Let cool. Reserve half of tomato fondue for sauce.

Cut four 17 × 17-inch sheets of parchment paper or aluminum foil. Fold each sheet in half, then unfold. Brush center of half of 1 sheet with melted butter. Place 1 teaspoon of remaining tomato fondue in center of buttered side. Top with fish fillet. Season with salt and pepper. Spread another teaspoon of fondue over fish. Fold unbuttered side over, then fold edges 3 times to seal papillote tightly. Repeat with remaining fish. Refrigerate papillotes.

For sauce: Combine wine, vinegar, shallot and preserved tarragon in heavy large saucepan over medium-high heat and cook until liquid is reduced to about 3 tablespoons. Let cool.

Meanwhile, melt remaining butter over low heat. Whisk yolks and water into cooled wine reduction. Place over low heat and whisk until thickened. Whisk butter into yolk mixture 1 drop at a time. Strain sauce through fine sieve. Blend in ½ teaspoon minced fresh tarragon leaves and reserved fondue (drain fondue first if too watery).

Preheat oven to 400°F. Arrange papillotes on baking sheet. Bake until very puffy, about 3 minutes. Serve in parchment. Pass sauce separately.

Striped Bass Livornese

6 to 8 servings

- 2 pounds striped bass or other firm white fish (steaks or thick fillets)
- ¼ cup all purpose flour
- ½ cup olive oil
- 1 small onion, sliced
- ¼ cup sliced pitted olives (both green and black)
- ¼ cup chopped oil-packed anchovy fillets
- 2 tablespoons capers, rinsed and drained
- 1 cup tomato sauce

  Minced fresh parsley (garnish)

Dredge fish lightly in flour. Heat most of olive oil in large skillet over medium heat. Add fish and sauté lightly on both sides. Remove fish and pour off oil. Wipe pan. Return fish to skillet and add remaining oil, onion, olives, anchovies and capers. Cover and simmer about 20 minutes. Add tomato sauce and cook until heated through and fish is opaque. Garnish with parsley.

🍒 Sashimi and Sushi

With today's trend toward simpler cooking, it is not surprising that Westerners are discovering the virtues of Japanese cuisine. The essence of Japanese cooking lies in its straightforward respect of the quality and beauty of ingredients. And in no branch of the cuisine are these principles more apparent than in the two seafood delicacies known as sashimi and sushi.

Sashimi is seafood at its simplest and most beautiful. Although uncooked, it has a subtle flavor that is anything but fishy. A wide variety of fish and shellfish may be used. *Maguro* (tuna), the most popular choice, has a deep pink color, clean flavor and a soft meaty texture. Very similar in flavor, though less rich, is pale yellow *hamachi* (yellowtail). *Suzuki* (sea bass), a mild-flavored white fish, is cut into a lovely paper-thin sashimi. Pale pink *hirame* (halibut) has a delicate flavor and is considered an excellent selection.

The same range of seafoods served as sashimi are transformed into sushi by the addition of vinegared rice and a dab of *wasabi*, a hot green horseradish paste. For all its diversity, sushi can be divided into three main types. *Nigir-izushi* are made by pressing fish, shellfish or roe onto a small oval of wasabi-seasoned rice. To create *oshizushi*, rice is pressed into a mold with marinated or boiled fish—usually mackerel—and then unmolded and sliced. For *mak-izushi*, thin strips of fish and vegetables are rolled in rice, wrapped in a crisp sheet of *nori* (dried seaweed) and cut into bite-sized rounds.

In preparing both sashimi and sushi, the Japanese chef combines the highest standards of quality with dexterity of hand and a keen artistic eye. After selecting only the very freshest seafood, he uses quick, clean knife strokes to slice each kind in a way that best complements its flavor and texture. These portions are then appropriately garnished in an elegant display that gives as much pleasure to the eye as it does to the palate.

🍒 Snapper

Cold Poached Snapper with Avocado Sauce

2 servings

2 red snapper or other firm-fleshed fish fillets (about ½ to ¾ pound total), room temperature
Salt and freshly ground pepper
½ cup dry white wine

1 medium avocado, peeled, pitted and coarsely chopped

2 tablespoons fresh lime juice
1 tablespoon grated onion
¼ teaspoon white wine vinegar
1½ tablespoons olive oil

Lime wedges and black olives (garnish)

Preheat oven to 400°F. Pat fish dry with paper towels. Place in small baking dish and sprinkle lightly with salt and pepper. Pour wine over. Cover dish with foil.

Bake 10 minutes for every inch of thickness of fish. Cool, then pour off poaching liquid (reserve for another use if desired). Cover; refrigerate until well chilled.

Combine avocado, lime juice, grated onion, vinegar and salt and pepper to taste in processor or blender. With machine running, slowly add olive oil in thin stream and mix until smooth, stopping as necessary to scrape down sides of container. Taste and adjust seasoning. Transfer sauce to small bowl, cover with plastic wrap and chill.

To serve, transfer fish to chilled plates. Spoon some of sauce onto each fillet. Garnish with lime wedges and olives.

Any extra sauce can be stored in tightly covered container in refrigerator. Thin slightly with oil and use as salad dressing.

Suprême of Red Snapper Duglère

A delicate white wine sauce tops the flaky red snapper. Serve with puff pastry crescents and boiled potatoes.

8 servings

¾ cup shallots, finely chopped
½ cup sliced mushrooms (optional)
8 6-ounce red snapper fillets
Salt and freshly ground white pepper

1 tablespoon butter
6 tomatoes, peeled, cored, seeded and coarsely chopped
¾ cup shallots, finely chopped
2 bay leaves
½ teaspoon dried thyme, crumbled
Salt and freshly ground pepper

4 cups (1 quart) Fish Fumet (see following recipe)
1 cup dry white wine
4 cups (1 quart) whipping cream

Fish Fumet (see following recipe)

Chopped fresh parsley (garnish)

Generously butter 2 large skillets. Sprinkle each with chopped shallot and sliced mushrooms. Arrange snapper in single layer in bottom of each skillet and season with salt and white pepper to taste. Set aside.

Melt butter in large saucepan over medium-low heat. Add tomatoes, remaining shallot, bay leaves, thyme, salt and pepper and sauté until liquid has evaporated, about 20 to 30 minutes. Remove from heat and set aside.

Reduce 4 cups fish fumet in medium saucepan over high heat until fumet is syrupy and coats bottom of pan. Meanwhile, pour wine into small saucepan and cook over medium-high heat until reduced to ⅓ cup. Cook whipping cream in large saucepan over medium-high heat until cream coats back of spoon. Blend fumet and wine into cream. Set sauce aside; keep warm.

Preheat oven to 375°F. Add enough fumet to snapper to cover. Cover skillets with parchment paper. Place over medium heat and bring to simmer. Transfer to oven and bake until fish is firm to touch, about 12 to 15 minutes. Drain well and arrange on individual plates. Blend white wine sauce into tomato mixture and spoon over fish, coating evenly. Garnish with parsley.

Fish Fumet

Makes about 1 quart

1 pound (about) fish trimmings (do
  not use salmon)
1 quart cold water
2 tablespoons tarragon vinegar
1 celery stalk (with leaves), cut into
  2-inch pieces
1 carrot, cut into 2-inch pieces

1 leek (white part only), split
¼ medium head of lettuce
5 white peppercorns
3 fresh dill sprigs
1 bay leaf
½ teaspoon dried thyme, crumbled
½ teaspoon salt

Combine all ingredients in 4- to 5-quart saucepan and bring to boil over medium-high heat. Reduce heat and simmer, uncovered, about 45 minutes. Strain through colander or cheesecloth-lined strainer before using.

Red Snapper Fillets with Herbs

4 first-course servings

½ to ¾ pound skinned red snapper
  fillets
  Olive oil
  Coarse salt
  Freshly ground white pepper

¼ cup packed fresh cilantro leaves
  (also known as coriander or
  Chinese parsley)

¼ cup packed fresh parsley leaves
2 tablespoons packed fresh mint
  leaves
3 tablespoons olive oil

1 teaspoon fresh lemon juice
¼ teaspoon coarse salt
  Freshly ground white pepper

Preheat oven to 450°F. Remove small bones from fillets with tweezers. Cut fillets on the diagonal, trimming each piece neatly to about 4½ by 2 inches. Lightly brush 4 ovenproof plates with olive oil and sprinkle lightly with salt and white pepper. Divide fish among plates, placing skinned side up in center. Brush lightly with olive oil. Sprinkle with salt and pepper. Press small piece of waxed paper on top of fish.

Finely chop herbs in processor or blender. With machine running, gradually add 3 tablespoons olive oil. Transfer to bowl.

Bake fish 5 to 8 minutes. Add lemon juice to herbs. Season with salt and pepper to taste.

Remove plates from oven, discard waxed paper and let plates stand 30 seconds. Spoon 2 teaspoons herb mixture along each side of fish. Serve.

Gruene Mansion

Serve with buttered rice.

6 servings

½ cup chopped green onion (white
  part only)
2 tablespoons plus 2 teaspoons
  minced fresh parsley
½ teaspoon ground rosemary
1 tablespoon olive oil
½ teaspoon salt

6 7½- to 8-ounce redfish or red
  snapper fillets

6 artichoke hearts, cooked and cut
  crosswise into 4 slices

Fish Fumet (see recipe, page 72)

3 limes, quartered (garnish)
  Fresh parsley (garnish)

Hollandaise sauce (optional)

Combine onion, parsley and rosemary in processor or blender and puree. Transfer to bowl. Whisk in oil and salt. Taste and adjust seasoning (there should be a hint of rosemary).

Preheat oven to 350°F. Arrange fillets in large shallow baking dish. Spread onion mixture over top. Decorate each fillet with 4 artichoke slices. Pour fish fumet into dish to depth of ¼ inch. Bake until fish appears flaky and white, about 15 to 20 minutes. Pour off any remaining liquid. Garnish fillets with lime and fresh parsley. Serve hot, with hollandaise sauce if desired.

Snapper in Cognac-Parmesan Sauce

12 servings

1 6-pound red snapper or striped bass, filleted
Juice of 3 lemons
2 small garlic cloves, minced
2 teaspoons salt or to taste
2 medium onions, chopped
1 tablespoon Matouk's pepper sauce* or other hot pepper sauce, or to taste
4 bay leaves, crumbled

1½ tablespoons oil
4 green onions, split

2 medium tomatoes, peeled and sliced or chopped
3 to 4 tablespoons butter
Parsley sprigs

4 ounces (½ cup) Cognac
6 tablespoons freshly grated Parmesan cheese

Whole green olives, capers and pimiento or red bell pepper strips (garnish)

Place fish in shallow baking pan. Squeeze lemon juice over and sprinkle with garlic and salt. Cover with onion, pepper sauce and bay leaves and marinate up to 2 days in refrigerator.

Preheat oven to 350°F. Drizzle fish with oil. Arrange green onion and tomatoes over and dot with butter. Add parsley sprigs. Cover and bake 30 minutes. Remove cover and continue baking about 15 minutes (allow 10 minutes for each 1-inch thickness of fish, measured at thickest part), until fish tests done.

Transfer fish to heated platter or large bowl and keep warm. Turn sauce into processor or blender, add Cognac and Parmesan and mix until smooth. Pour over fish. Garnish with olives, capers and pimiento or red pepper strips.

*Available in Spanish, Indonesian or Indian specialty food stores.

Plantation Gardens Red Snapper

6 servings

½ cup dry white wine
½ onion, thinly sliced
1 bay leaf
Pinch of dried thyme, crumbled
½ cup whipping cream
½ cup (1 stick) butter, cut into pieces
½ garlic clove, crushed
1 small slice fresh ginger, peeled and minced
2 sprigs fresh parsley, finely chopped

½ teaspoon soy sauce
Salt and freshly ground pepper

1 tablespoon butter
6 3½- to 4-ounce red snapper fillets

Watercress sprigs (garnish)
Lemon wedges and chopped fresh parsley (garnish)

Combine wine, onion, bay leaf and thyme in medium saucepan and bring to boil over medium-high heat. Continue cooking until liquid is almost evaporated. Reduce heat, add cream and simmer until mixture coats spoon, about 2 minutes. Press through strainer and return to saucepan. Stir in ½ cup butter, blending thoroughly. Add garlic, ginger, parsley and soy sauce. Taste and season with salt and pepper.

Melt remaining butter in heavy skillet over medium heat. Sprinkle fillets with salt and pepper. Add to skillet and fry on both sides until fillets are lightly browned and cooked through. Transfer to heated plate.

Arrange watercress on serving platter. Reheat sauce gently, adding any juices accumulated around fish. Cook until slightly thickened. Arrange fillets on watercress and top with sauce. Garnish with lemon and parsley. Serve immediately.

Red Snapper Szechwan

6 to 8 servings

1 tablespoon Shaohsing rice wine*
   or dry Sherry
½ egg, lightly beaten
¼ teaspoon salt
⅛ teaspoon freshly ground pepper
¾ pound red snapper fillets

1½ tablespoons chopped green onion
4 teaspoons fermented black beans*
1 tablespoon chopped fresh ginger
1 tablespoon chopped garlic
1½ teaspoons Szechwan chili paste*
¾ cup chicken or vegetable stock or Fish Fumet (see recipe, page 72)
⅓ cup soy sauce
3 tablespoons Shaohsing rice wine or dry Sherry
2½ tablespoons sugar
2 tablespoons rice vinegar

1 teaspoon salt
1 tablespoon cornstarch
1 tablespoon water

6 cups oil
2 cups cornstarch
¼ head cabbage, cut into 1-inch cubes (4 ounces)
1 small onion, cut into 1-inch cubes (2 ounces)
1 green bell pepper, cored, seeded, deveined and cut into 1-inch squares

2 tablespoons oil
   Freshly cooked rice

Combine 1 tablespoon wine with egg, salt and pepper in large bowl and blend well. Cut snapper fillets crosswise into 1½ × 1 × ¼-inch pieces. Add to wine mixture, tossing to coat. Marinate for at least 1 hour.

Combine green onion, black beans, ginger, garlic and chili paste in cup. Blend stock, soy sauce, 3 tablespoons wine, sugar, vinegar and salt in bowl. Mix 1 tablespoon cornstarch with water in another cup.

Heat 6 cups oil in wok or large saucepan to 375°F. Combine fish and 2 cups cornstarch in large bowl or bag and toss to coat completely. Transfer to metal strainer and shake to remove all excess cornstarch. Lower strainer into hot oil and fry fish until crisp and lightly browned, 45 seconds to 1 minute. Remove strainer and drain fish well. Add cabbage, onion and green pepper to oil and fry 10 seconds. Remove vegetables and drain well. Discard oil; wipe out wok.

Pour 2 tablespoons oil into wok and place over high heat. Add black bean mixture and stir vigorously for several seconds. Add stock mixture, stir through and bring to boil. As soon as sauce boils, add cornstarch mixture and blend well. When sauce returns to boil, add fish and vegetables and stir to coat. Serve immediately with rice.

*Available at oriental markets.

Red Snapper en Croûte with Lobster Sauce

8 servings

Lobster Sauce
½ cup (1 stick) unsalted butter
1 lobster shell, broken up
⅓ cup chopped onion
⅓ cup chopped carrot
1 cup chopped tomato
½ cup (or more) brandy

2 cups Fish Fumet (see recipe, page 72)
1 tablespoon all purpose flour
1 cup white wine
Pinch of dried tarragon, crumbled
Salt and freshly ground white pepper

1 cup whipping cream

Snapper en Croûte
6 tablespoons (¾ stick) unsalted butter
8 6-ounce red snapper fillets, room temperature
Salt and freshly ground white pepper

2 pounds Classic Puff Pastry (see recipe, page 38)
2 cups Duxelles (see following recipe)
1 egg, beaten

For sauce: Melt butter in large saucepan or Dutch oven over medium heat. Add lobster shell, onion and carrot. Increase heat to high and cook about 2 minutes, stirring. Add tomato and ½ cup brandy and ignite, shaking pan gently until flame subsides. Remove from heat and set aside.

Place ¼ cup fish fumet in small bowl. Add flour, whisking to remove all lumps. Add to tomato mixture and blend well. Pour remaining 1¾ cups fish fumet into small saucepan. Place over high heat and bring to boil. Add to tomato mixture with wine, tarragon, salt and pepper. Place over medium-low heat and simmer about 20 minutes.

Discard lobster shell. Strain liquid through very fine sieve into another saucepan. Add cream. Place over medium heat and boil slowly until sauce is reduced enough to coat spoon, about 20 minutes. Taste and adjust seasoning. Keep sauce warm.

For snapper: Melt butter in 10-inch skillet over medium-high heat. Sprinkle both sides of fillets with salt and pepper. Add fillets to skillet and sauté not more than 1 minute on each side. Remove from heat and cool.

Cut puff pastry in half. Roll half of dough out on floured surface to thickness of ⅛ inch. Arrange fillets on dough, spacing at least 1 inch apart. Spread each fillet with some of duxelles, smoothing over entire surface. Trim excess puff pastry around each fillet, leaving about ½-inch border on all sides. Brush border with beaten egg.

Preheat oven to 375°F. Butter shallow large baking pan. Roll remaining puff pastry ⅛ inch thick and cut into 8 pieces to top fillets and come down sides to seal with bottom pastry. Press gently around edges to seal each fillet in dough. Trim edges if necessary. Transfer to prepared pan. Brush puff pastry with beaten egg. Bake until golden brown, about 20 minutes. Transfer to heated platter. Taste sauce and add more brandy if desired. Cut opening in each top crust and pour in 1 to 2 tablespoons sauce. Pass remaining sauce separately.

Duxelles

Makes 2 cups

¼ cup (½ stick) unsalted butter
2 tablespoons oil
¼ cup minced shallot or white part of green onion
2 pounds mushrooms, minced

½ cup Madeira, Port or white or red wine (optional)
2 tablespoons fresh lemon juice
¼ teaspoon freshly grated nutmeg
Salt and freshly ground pepper

Melt butter with oil in heavy large skillet over low heat. Add shallot and stir constantly until translucent. Add mushrooms and cook, stirring frequently to prevent sticking, until pieces are dark and begin to dry, about 20 minutes. Add wine and continue cooking over low heat until liquid has almost completely evaporated, about 1 hour. Season with lemon juice, nutmeg, and salt and freshly ground pepper to taste.

❦ Sole

Basic Poached Sole Fillets

Save the cooking liquid for a good fish-flavored concentrate or stock to use in an accompanying sauce.

4 to 6 servings

4 to 6 medium to large sole fillets
Fresh lemon juice

2 tablespoons light vegetable oil (preferably cold-pressed safflower) or unsalted butter
1 small onion, sliced

1¼ cups clam juice
1 tablespoon fresh lemon juice
1 bay leaf
1 garlic clove, crushed
6 peppercorns

Preheat oven to 350°F. Pat fillets dry. Sprinkle with fresh lemon juice. Roll up fillets, skin side in, and fasten with toothpicks. Set aside.

Heat oil in small flameproof baking dish over medium-high heat. Add onion and sauté 2 minutes. Add clam juice, 1 tablespoon fresh lemon juice, bay leaf, garlic and peppercorns and bring to boil. Add fillets. Cover with sheet of greased waxed paper. Transfer to oven and bake just until fish turns opaque, about 5 to 8 minutes. Immediately transfer fillets to serving platter using long, wide spatula. Strain cooking liquid and reserve for another use.

Sautéed Sole Fillets with Fines Herbes

4 servings

2 tablespoons (¼ stick) unsalted butter
1 shallot or pearl onion, finely chopped
1 teaspoon chopped chives
1 tablespoon chopped fresh parsley
1 teaspoon chopped fresh tarragon or ¼ teaspoon dried, crumbled
1 teaspoon chopped chervil
1 teaspoon fresh lemon juice
Freshly ground white pepper
Herb or vegetable salt (optional)

8 small sole fillets
Fresh lemon juice
Freshly ground white pepper
Whole wheat pastry flour
1 egg, lightly beaten
½ cup (about) dry whole wheat breadcrumbs
¼ cup light vegetable oil (preferably cold-pressed safflower)

Lemon wedges (garnish)
Parsley sprigs (garnish)

Melt butter in medium skillet over medium heat. Add shallot and cook, stirring constantly, until tender, about 3 minutes. Reduce heat to low, add chives and cook, stirring constantly, 2 minutes. Add parsley, tarragon and chervil and continue cooking 1 minute, stirring constantly. Stir in 1 teaspoon lemon juice. Season with white pepper and herb salt. Set aside.

Pat fillets dry with paper towels. Fold fillets in half lengthwise. Sprinkle with lemon juice and pepper and dust lightly with whole wheat pastry flour. Brush with beaten egg and roll in breadcrumbs. Heat oil in large skillet over high heat. Add fillets (in batches if necessary) and brown lightly on each side. Transfer to paper towels using long, wide spatula and drain. Arrange fillets on warm serving platter. Spread herb mixture over each fillet. Garnish with lemon wedges and parsley and serve.

Fillet of Sole in Tarragon Butter

3 to 4 servings

2 tablespoons (¼ stick) butter
¼ pound mushrooms, sliced
1 small onion, chopped
1 pound sole fillets

¼ cup dry vermouth
Butter
1½ teaspoons dried tarragon
Salt and freshly ground pepper

Preheat oven to 350°F. Line 9 × 13-inch baking dish with foil. Melt butter in medium skillet over medium-high heat. Add mushrooms and onion and sauté until softened, about 5 minutes. Arrange fillets in dish. Pour vermouth over fish. Dot each piece with butter and sprinkle with tarragon, salt and pepper. Spoon mushroom mixture evenly over top. Cover with foil and bake until fish loses its translucency, about 30 minutes.

Sole Fillets with Buttered Ginger Sauce

3 to 4 first-course servings

¾ to 1 pound sole fillets
Melted butter
Coarse salt
Freshly ground white pepper

Fresh Ginger Sauce
¾ cup water
½ cup julienne of peeled fresh ginger
⅓ cup sugar

1 cup dry white wine

5 tablespoons unsalted butter, cut into ½-inch pieces
1½ teaspoons fresh lemon juice
Coarse salt and freshly ground white pepper

12 small melon balls (garnish)
4 mint sprigs (garnish)

Remove small bones from fillets with tweezers. Cut fillets on the diagonal, trimming each piece neatly to about 4½ × 2 inches. Lightly brush 4 ovenproof plates with melted butter and sprinkle lightly with salt and white pepper. Arrange fish in center of each plate. Brush lightly with butter and sprinkle with salt and pepper. Press small piece of waxed paper on top of fish. Set aside while preparing sauce.

For sauce: Combine water, ginger and sugar in heavy 2-quart saucepan. Place over medium-low heat and stir until sugar is dissolved. Cover and continue cooking 30 minutes. Uncover, increase heat and cook until liquid is reduced to about ¼ cup. Add wine and continue cooking until liquid is reduced to ¼ cup. Remove sauce from heat and discard about half of ginger.

Preheat oven to 450°F. Whisk butter into sauce 1 piece at a time, making sure each piece is fully incorporated before adding the next (return pan to low heat if necessary). Stir in lemon juice, salt and freshly ground white pepper. Set aside and keep warm.

Bake fish 3 minutes. Remove plates from oven and let stand 30 seconds. Discard waxed paper. Spoon 1 to 1½ tablespoons sauce over each piece of fish. Place melon balls and mint sprigs on left side of each plate and serve.

Ceviche

2 servings

¾ pound sole fillets, cut into ½-inch strips
¾ cup fresh lime juice
¼ cup olive oil
½ garlic clove, minced
3 tablespoons chopped fresh parsley
2 tablespoons chopped green onion
1 tablespoon diced green chilies

¾ teaspoon salt
¼ teaspoon freshly ground pepper
Dash of hot pepper sauce
Lettuce leaves

1 medium avocado, peeled, halved, pitted and sliced (garnish)

Arrange fish in single layer in small baking dish. Pour lime juice over top. Cover and marinate at room temperature, turning occasionally, about 1 hour. Meanwhile, combine oil, garlic, parsley, green onion, chilies, salt, pepper and hot pepper sauce in small bowl and mix well. Drain fish well. Return to dish. Pour oil mixture over fish and toss gently. Let stand 30 minutes. Arrange lettuce leaves on platter. Top with fish and garnish with avocado slices. Serve immediately.

Oven-Poached Sole with Vegetables

4 servings

4 canned plum tomatoes, drained and sliced
5 garlic cloves, crushed
½ medium onion, thinly sliced
3 tablespoons dry vermouth
1 teaspoon *each* chopped fresh tarragon and fresh thyme or scant ¼ teaspoon *each* dried, crumbled
4 6-ounce (about) sole fillets

3 tablespoons Spanish Sherry wine vinegar
1¼ cups Lean Fish Fumet (see recipe, page 33)

1 teaspoon whipped unsalted butter
2 small turnips, cut into fine julienne
2 small carrots, cut into fine julienne
½ medium onion, thinly slivered
2 small zucchini, cut into fine julienne
8 snow peas, cut into fine julienne

Salt and freshly ground pepper

Combine tomatoes, garlic, sliced onion, vermouth, tarragon and thyme in 8 × 10-inch baking dish. Fold fillets in half crosswise and arrange in single layer in dish. Spoon vermouth mixture over. Cover and refrigerate 1 hour.

Preheat oven to 375°F. Sprinkle fillets with vinegar. Bring fish fumet to gentle simmer in medium saucepan over medium heat. Pour over fillets. Cover dish with heavy foil, sealing edges well. Bake until fillets are barely firm to touch, about 10 to 15 minutes.

Meanwhile, melt butter in large skillet over high heat. Add turnip, carrot and slivered onion and stir-fry until barely tender, about 1 minute. Add zucchini and snow peas and stir-fry until crisp-tender, about 30 seconds. Remove skillet from heat and set aside.

Transfer fish to ovenproof platter using slotted spatula. Turn off oven. Set fish in oven with door ajar. Pour poaching liquid into medium saucepan. Place over medium-high heat and bring to boil. Let boil until reduced by ⅔. Transfer mixture to processor or blender and puree. Add salt and pepper to taste. Divide sauce evenly among 4 heated serving plates. Top with fillets. Quickly rewarm vegetables over high heat. Sprinkle evenly over fish fillets. Serve immediately.

Poached Sole Fillets with Asparagus

4 servings

12 medium-size fresh asparagus tips
4 tablespoons (½ stick) unsalted butter
1 tablespoon whole wheat pastry flour
⅔ cup reserved sole cooking liquid (see recipe for Basic Poached Sole Fillets, page 66)
½ cup half and half

Ground red pepper to taste
Herb or vegetable salt (optional)
2 tablespoons whipping cream

4 medium to large sole fillets, poached (see recipe for Basic Poached Sole Fillets)

Steam asparagus tips until crisp-tender, about 4 minutes. Drain and split in half lengthwise; set aside. Melt 2 tablespoons butter in medium saucepan over medium-low heat. Add flour and cook 3 minutes, stirring constantly. Pour in reserved cooking liquid and half and half. Bring to boil over medium-high heat, stirring constantly. Reduce heat to low and season with ground red pepper and herb salt. Stir in remaining 2 tablespoons butter 1 tablespoon at a time. Add whipping cream and reserved asparagus tips.

Preheat broiler. Arrange poached sole fillets in baking dish. Pour sauce over. Run under broiler until top is lightly browned. Serve immediately.

Sole Fillets with Mushrooms and Apples Steamed in Paper

6 servings

8 medium sole fillets
11 medium-size fresh mushrooms (2 finely chopped; 9 thinly sliced)
3 tablespoons sour cream
1 tablespoon finely chopped fresh parsley
2 teaspoons fresh lemon juice
2 teaspoons chopped fresh tarragon or ½ teaspoon dried, crumbled
1 teaspoon finely chopped garlic
1 egg white
Fresh lemon juice
6 tablespoons (¾ stick) unsalted butter

1 teaspoon lemon juice
Freshly ground white pepper
Herb or vegetable salt (optional)
2 medium-size tart apples, peeled, cored and coarsely chopped
1 tablespoon chopped chives

Pat fillets dry with paper towels. Cut 2 fillets into 1-inch strips and transfer to processor; set remaining fillets aside. Add 2 chopped mushrooms, sour cream, parsley, 2 teaspoons lemon juice, 1 teaspoon fresh tarragon or ¼ teaspoon dried, ½ teaspoon garlic and egg white to processor and mix until well blended. Arrange remaining 6 fillets skin side up on work surface. Sprinkle with lemon juice. Top each fillet with spoonful of mushroom mixture and fold over, end to end. Melt 2 tablespoons butter and brush over each fillet. Cut six 12-inch squares of aluminum foil or parchment paper. Arrange folded fillets on foil or parchment squares.

Melt 1 tablespoon butter in small skillet over high heat. Add 9 sliced mushrooms, 1 teaspoon lemon juice, pepper and herb salt and sauté 2 minutes, stirring constantly. Spread layer of mushrooms over each fillet. Melt 1 tablespoon butter in same skillet over high heat. Add apple and sauté 1 to 2 minutes, stirring constantly. Spread apple over mushrooms. Combine remaining 2 tablespoons butter, remaining ½ teaspoon garlic, remaining 1 teaspoon fresh or ¼ teaspoon dried tarragon, chives, pepper and herb salt in small bowl and beat well. Top each fillet with generous spoonful of herb mixture.

Preheat oven to 350°F. Fold foil over each fillet so corners meet in triangle. Roll edges of foil to seal tightly. Arrange fish packages on jelly roll pan or baking sheet and bake 20 to 25 minutes. Carefully cut slit in center of each package and serve immediately.

Double Sole Spinach Soufflé and Spinach Crepe Paupiette

If you have no fish fumet on hand for sauce, substitute liquid squeezed from cooked spinach.

2 to 4 servings

Crepes (10 to 12 6½-inch crepes)
- ½ cup flour
- 1 cup milk, room temperature
- 2 eggs, lightly beaten
- ½ teaspoon salt
- ⅛ teaspoon freshly ground pepper
  Pinch of freshly ground nutmeg

- 1 large bunch (about 1 pound) spinach, stems removed

- 3 tablespoons butter

Soufflé
- 1 tablespoon whipping cream
- 1 egg yolk
  Salt and freshly ground pepper
  Freshly ground nutmeg
  Squeeze of lemon juice
- 2 egg whites, room temperature

Pinch of salt
Pinch of cream of tartar

- 4 sole fillets (1 pound total)
  Salt and freshly ground pepper
  Juice of ½ lemon

Sauce
- 3 egg yolks
- ½ cup whipping cream
- ½ cup Fish Fumet (see recipe, page 72)
  Salt and freshly ground pepper
  Juice of ½ lemon
- 1 tablespoon freshly snipped chives
- 2 tablespoons chilled butter, chopped

For crepes: Place flour in bowl. Pour in about ⅓ cup milk, a little at a time, stirring constantly with whisk to make smooth paste. Gradually whisk in remaining milk and eggs. Season to taste with salt, pepper and nutmeg. If there are any lumps, pass through sieve. Cover bowl lightly and let batter rest at room temperature for at least 1 hour.

Meanwhile, prepare spinach. Wash leaves and shake dry. Place in heavy-bottomed skillet and stir over high heat until wilted. Reduce heat, cover and cook for 5 minutes, stirring occasionally. Cool. Squeeze dry with hands (reserve liquid for sauce, if needed). Chop spinach coarsely. Stir half into crepe mixture, reserving remainder for soufflé.

Melt butter in crepe pan. Cool. Stir about 1 tablespoon of butter into crepe batter, mixing well. Clarify remaining butter and pour into small glass.

Heat crepe pan over medium-high heat. Brush with clarified butter and heat until almost smoking. Remove pan from heat, ladle about 3 tablespoons of batter into one corner of pan, then tilt pan in all directions until bottom is evenly covered with thin layer of batter. Pour out any excess.

Return pan to medium-high heat. Loosen edges of crepe with small spatula or tip of knife and cook for about 1 minute until bottom of crepe is brown, shaking pan in circle so crepe doesn't stick. Flip or turn crepe over with spatula and cook another minute until second side is brown. *(The crepe pan is too cool if edges of crepes don't begin coloring immediately; it is too hot if holes form as soon as batter is poured in.)* Slide crepe out onto a plate. Repeat with remaining batter. When cool, cover crepes with plastic wrap. Refrigerate or freeze if not using crepes same day.

For soufflé: Puree reserved spinach in processor or blender with cream and egg yolk. Season to taste with salt, pepper, nutmeg and lemon juice. Just before using, beat egg whites with salt and cream of tartar until stiff. Carefully fold egg whites into spinach.

Preheat oven to 375°F. Butter 9 × 13-inch baking dish. Sprinkle both sides of sole fillets with salt, pepper and lemon juice. Place skinned side up. Divide soufflé mixture among sole fillets, spreading evenly and leaving ½-inch border all around. Gently roll up and arrange seam side down in baking dish. Cover with buttered parchment paper and bake until fillets are just opaque, about 10 minutes. Wrap at least 8 crepes in foil and reheat with fish.

For sauce: Combine egg yolks, cream and fish fumet (or liquid from spinach) in heavy-bottomed saucepan and whisk over low heat until thickened. Season to taste with salt, pepper, lemon juice and chives. Whisk in 2 tablespoons butter just before serving.

Overlap 2 crepes on heated plate, turning so least attractive side is facing up. Spread some sauce over crepes. Place a sole fillet in center where 2 crepes overlap. Spoon some sauce over sole. Roll crepes up and turn seam side down. Repeat with remaining crepes. Serve immediately with remaining sauce.

Sautéed Fillets of Sole St. Tropez

4 servings

2 tablespoons light vegetable oil (preferably cold-pressed safflower) or unsalted butter
1 medium-size yellow onion, finely chopped
2½ cups finely chopped fresh mushrooms
⅓ cup finely chopped shallot
1 tablespoon finely chopped fresh parsley
1 tablespoon chopped fresh tarragon or ½ teaspoon dried, crumbled
1 teaspoon finely chopped chives
1 teaspoon finely chopped garlic
Herb or vegetable salt (optional)

Cheese Velouté Sauce
2 tablespoons light vegetable oil (preferably cold-pressed safflower) or unsalted butter
2 tablespoons whole wheat pastry flour
1 cup Fish Fumet (see following recipe) *or* bottled clam juice
½ cup freshly grated Parmesan cheese
1 cup whipping cream or sour cream
Ground red pepper
Herb or vegetable salt (optional)

8 small or 4 large sole fillets
Fresh lemon juice
¼ cup (about) milk
Whole wheat pastry flour
¼ cup plus 1 tablespoon light vegetable oil

Heat 2 tablespoons oil in medium skillet over medium heat. Add onion and cook about 10 minutes or until tender. Add mushrooms, shallot, parsley, tarragon, chives and garlic and stir through. Season with herb salt if desired. Increase heat to high and cook, stirring constantly, 4 to 5 minutes. Reduce heat to low and cook, stirring occasionally, 5 minutes. Set aside.

For sauce: Heat 2 tablespoons oil in medium saucepan over medium-low heat. Whisk in flour and cook, stirring constantly, 3 minutes. Add fish fumet. Increase heat to medium high and bring to boil, stirring constantly. Add ¼ cup Parmesan and bring to boil again. Stir in cream, ground red pepper and herb salt and bring to boil, stirring constantly. Remove from heat.

Pat fillets dry with paper towels. Fold fillets in half lengthwise, skin side in. Sprinkle with lemon juice, brush with milk and sprinkle lightly with whole wheat pastry flour. Heat ¼ cup oil in large skillet over high heat. Add fillets (in batches if necessary) and brown lightly on each side, being careful not to overcook. Transfer to warm flameproof serving dish.

Preheat broiler. Spread herb mixture over fillets. Cover with sauce. Sprinkle remaining ¼ cup Parmesan over sauce and drizzle with remaining 1 tablespoon oil. Brown fillets lightly under broiler and serve immediately.

Fish Fumet

Makes 1 cup

Fish head and bones
2 cups water
½ cup mixed sliced carrot, sliced celery and sliced onion

1 bay leaf
6 peppercorns

Combine fish head and bones, water, vegetables, bay leaf and peppercorns in medium saucepan. Bring to boil. Reduce heat and simmer 20 minutes. Strain well; discard bones, vegetables and seasoning. Return liquid to saucepan. Place over high heat and boil until liquid is reduced to 1 cup.

Fumet can be doubled or tripled. Any extra can be frozen up to 1 month.

Stuffed Sole Florentine

Many restaurant chefs use a lobster and scallop stock to make the sauce for this dish, but the fish-poaching liquid makes an excellent substitute.

4 servings

1½ teaspoons butter
6 oysters, shucked, drained and coarsely chopped (¾ cup)
½ medium onion, finely chopped
1½ tablespoons dry Sherry
1 tablespoon Worcestershire sauce
2 garlic cloves, chopped
¾ teaspoon salt
⅛ teaspoon freshly ground pepper
Pinch of freshly ground white pepper
5 ounces fresh spinach, rinsed, dried and stemmed (4 cups packed leaves)
3 tablespoons (about) dried breadcrumbs
½ lightly beaten egg

8 3-ounce sole fillets
2 tablespoons (¼ stick) butter, melted
¼ cup (about) Rhine wine
¼ cup (about) clam juice

1½ cups whipping cream
1 egg yolk
¼ cup (½ stick) unsalted butter (well chilled), cut into ½-inch pieces

Paprika

Lemon wedges and parsley sprigs (garnish)

Melt 1½ teaspoons butter in large skillet over medium heat. Add oyster, onion, Sherry, Worcestershire, garlic and seasoning and bring to simmer. Let simmer until most of liquid is evaporated, about 6 to 8 minutes. Transfer to large bowl. Stir in spinach. Chop mixture finely or pass through coarse blade of food grinder. Stir in enough breadcrumbs to absorb any remaining moisture. Blend in egg.

Preheat oven to 450°F. Spread each fillet with about 2 tablespoons spinach mixture and roll up to enclose filling. Butter baking dish just large enough to accommodate fish. Arrange fillets in prepared dish. Brush with melted butter. Add enough wine and clam juice (in equal proportions) to come halfway up fish. Cover with foil and bake until fish is opaque and internal temperature reaches 150°F, about 20 minutes. Drain poaching liquid into medium saucepan. Set sole fillets aside and keep warm.

Boil poaching liquid over medium-high heat until reduced to ½ cup. Reduce heat, add cream and simmer until thickened (sauce should be consistency of heavy pancake batter). Remove from heat. Whisk in egg yolk. Gradually add ¼ cup chilled unsalted butter, whisking constantly.

Arrange fillets on heated platter. Ladle sauce around fish, spooning small amount atop each fillet. Sprinkle with paprika. Garnish with lemon wedges and parsley and serve.

Sole Wellington

6 servings

Butter
2 tablespoons (¼ stick) butter
1¼ cups sliced mushrooms
½ cup diced shallot
6 green onions, chopped
½ cup dry white wine
2 cups cooked chopped tiny shrimp
⅓ cup chopped fresh cilantro (also known as coriander or Chinese parsley)
½ cup whipping cream

2 teaspoons beurre manié (1 teaspoon butter mixed with 1 teaspoon flour)
Salt and freshly ground pepper

6 sole fillets (about 5 to 6 ounces each), skinned
6 6-inch squares puff pastry (⅛ to ¼ inch thick)
1 egg, beaten
Béarnaise sauce

Line baking pan with parchment paper. Butter paper. Melt 2 tablespoons butter in medium saucepan over medium-high heat. Add mushrooms, shallot and green onion and sauté 6 to 7 minutes. Add wine, increase heat to high and cook, stirring frequently, until mixture is reduced to 3 tablespoons, about 3 to 4 minutes. Add shrimp and cilantro and cook, stirring frequently, 1 to 2 minutes. Reduce heat and blend in cream. Gradually add beurre manié, stirring until thickened. Season to taste with salt and pepper. Remove from heat and set aside to cool.

Preheat oven to 375°F. Spoon 3½ to 4 ounces of filling over each fillet. Roll up securely. Set each in center of pastry square. Fold pastry over fish envelope style, moistening edges with beaten egg to seal. Brush pastry with remaining egg. Transfer to prepared pan. Bake until pastry is golden brown, about 20 to 30 minutes. Serve immediately with béarnaise sauce.

🍎 *Poaching Fish*

Nothing makes a more impressive centerpiece for a summer buffet than a poached fish, whether decorated simply with herbs and lemon or resplendent in a delicate coat of overlapping cucumber slices. Gentle poaching in a small amount of liquid seals in the flavor, keeping the fish moist and flavorful—a simple procedure that can be used to cook any find of fish.

The traditional poaching liquid is court bouillon, a combination of water, wine, vegetables, herbs and seasonings. Fish bones, heads and tails, if available (your fish merchant may be able to supply you with trimmings), enrich the flavor. Poached fish may be served hot or cold, plain or with sauces.

We have provided a recipe for classic court bouillon, as well as a simpler version made with clam juice.

Poached Fish

About 4 servings

- 2 quarts (8 cups) cold water
- 1 tablespoon salt *or* 2 tablespoons lemon juice
- 1 3- to 5-pound whole fish, filleted, head and tail removed if desired (reserve bones and trimmings)
- Court Bouillon or Easy Court Bouillon (see following recipes)

Combine water with salt or lemon juice. Rinse fish fillets in this liquid. Do not rinse under running water or valuable enzymes will wash away.

Wrap each fillet in cheesecloth or a cloth towel (not terry). Twist ends of fabric and tie with string. This retains original shape of fish and makes fillets easy to handle.

Place fillet on top of one another in fish poacher or roasting pan. Arrange 2 wrapped fillets facing in opposite directions so thickness of fish is evenly distributed. Cover with cold Court Bouillon (add water if Court Bouillon is insufficient to cover) and place over 2 burners. Bring Court Bouillon to a boil, cover and reduce heat to simmer. Poach fish approximately 5 to 8 minutes per pound, depending on thickness of fillets, until it loses its translucency and can just be flaked with a fork. Be careful not to poach too long, as fish will continue to cook after it has been removed from heat.

If serving hot: Cover fish and allow to stand in Court Bouillon at room temperature 10 minutes after cooking.

If serving cold: Cover fish and allow to stand in Court Bouillon at room temperature until completely cooled.

When ready to remove fish from Court Bouillon, lift each fillet from liquid, using ends of twisted cheesecloth as handles. Allow liquid to drip back into poacher. Unwrap but do not remove cheesecloth. With a small knife, peel off skin from tail to gill. Using cheesecloth, flip each fillet onto a serving platter. If serving chilled, cover and refrigerate.

Serve chilled with plain or flavored mayonnaise or cucumber sauce, or hot with hollandaise or sauce beurre blanc.

🍎

Court Bouillon

Makes about 2 quarts

2 quarts (8 cups) cold water
2 cups dry white wine
¼ cup tarragon vinegar
2 celery stalks, including leaves, cut into 2-inch pieces
2 carrots, cut into 2-inch pieces
½ medium heat lettuce, cut into chunks
2 leeks, white part only, *or* 1 large onion, peeled and sliced

2 bay leaves
1 teaspoon thyme
1 teaspoon salt, or to taste
10 whole peppercorns
5 sprigs fresh dill or ½ teaspoon dried dillweed
3 sprigs parsley
1 lemon, thinly sliced
Fish trimmings (optional)

Combine all ingredients in 5- or 6-quart pot. Bring to boil, reduce heat and simmer uncovered 45 minutes. Strain through cheesecloth. Cool.

Easy Court Bouillon

Makes 6 to 7 cups

4 8-ounce bottles clam juice
1 quart (4 cups) water
2 cups dry white wine
1 lemon, thinly sliced, seeds removed

1 celery stalk, including leaves, cut into 2-inch pieces
1 onion, peeled and halved
2 carrots, cut into 2-inch pieces
3 fresh parsley sprigs

Combine all ingredients in 4- or 5-quart saucepan and bring to a boil. Reduce heat and simmer uncovered until liquid has been reduced by ⅓.

Variation

Poaching Fish Steaks: Rinse salmon, swordfish, halibut or other fish steaks in salted or acidulated water. Place in a 10- or 12-inch skillet or fish poacher and add simmering Court Bouillon to cover. Butter a waxed paper circle and place buttered side down on fish. (This keeps flavors from evaporating and enables you to see and control simmering.) Cook until fish loses its translucency and flakes with a fork. Lift steaks from pan with spatula. Place on platter and blot up excess liquids.

Great Hints

- A variety of garnishes can be used to dress up a poached fish: parsley sprigs, radish roses, turnip daisies, lemon twists, pimiento, fresh dill, lemon or tomato roses. Or create a coat of cucumber scales: Scrub small pickling cucumbers thoroughly, then slice unpeeled cucumbers thinly (a swiveled potato peeler is handy for this) and arrange slices atop fish, overlapping to resemble scales.
- If you do not own two platters large enough to hold the fish fillets, cover a cookie sheet with foil. Place the fish on pan diagonally, and cover exposed surface of foil with garnishes.
- Court Bouillon may be frozen and reused again and again. Court Bouillon used for poaching salmon should not be used for poaching other kinds of fish.

🐛 *Swordfish*

Swordfish Steak with Lemon and Capers

6 servings

3 to 4 lemons

6 slices swordfish (about 8 ounces each)
Salt and freshly ground white pepper
Milk
All purpose flour

12 tablespoons peanut oil
1 teaspoon butter

5 tablespoons unsalted butter
¼ cup drained capers

2 tablespoons chopped fresh parsley (garnish)

Carefully peel lemons, discarding all of white pith. Cut white membrane from lemon sections. Remove segments, then dice.

Generously season swordfish with salt and white pepper. Dip each slice in milk. Coat with flour, shaking off excess.

Heat 6 tablespoons oil in large skillet over medium-high heat. Stir in ½ teaspoon butter. Add 3 slices of fish and sauté until lightly browned on both sides. Reduce heat and continue cooking until fish is opaque and feels firm to touch. Transfer to heated serving platter and keep warm. Repeat with remaining oil, ½ teaspoon butter and fish.

Wipe out skillet. Add remaining 5 tablespoons butter and cook over medium heat until lightly browned. Stir in reserved lemon and capers. Pour over fish, garnish with chopped parsley and serve immediately.

Capered Swordfish Steaks

Succulent swordfish steaks are baked on a bed of aromatic vegetables accented with lemon, capers and dry white wine. Boiled new potatoes tossed with butter and parsley are an excellent accompaniment. Halibut or salmon steaks may also be done in this manner.

4 servings

½ cup (1 stick) butter
¾ cup minced onion
¾ cup minced carrot
¾ cup minced fennel or celery
½ to ¾ cup peeled, seeded and chopped lemon
3 tablespoons capers, rinsed and drained
Salt and freshly ground pepper

4 8-ounce swordfish steaks, 1 inch thick
Salt and freshly ground white pepper
2 lemons, thinly sliced
4 tablespoons (½ stick) butter
¾ cup dry white wine

Minced fresh dillweed (garnish)

Preheat oven to 350°F. Melt ½ cup butter in large skillet over medium heat. Add onion and sauté until limp and transparent, about 5 minutes; *do not brown.* Increase heat to medium-high, add carrot, fennel or celery and lemon and sauté until mixture is thick and glazed, about 10 to 12 minutes. Add capers and sauté an additional minute. Season with salt and pepper.

Turn into large shallow baking dish, spreading evenly to cover bottom.

Rinse fish and pat dry with paper towels. Arrange in single layer atop vegetables. Sprinkle with salt and white pepper. Place lemon slices over steaks and top each steak with 1 tablespoon butter. Pour wine over fish and vegetables. Cover dish tightly with foil and bake 20 minutes. Remove foil and bake an additional 5 to 10 minutes, or until fish flakes when touched lightly with fork. Transfer fish and vegetables to heated platter and dust with dill.

Zesty Grilled Swordfish

4 servings

1 pound swordfish fillets, boned and cut into 1-inch pieces
2 tablespoons soy sauce
2 tablespoons orange juice
1 tablespoon oil
1 tablespoon catsup
1 tablespoon chopped fresh parsley

1 small garlic clove, chopped
½ teaspoon fresh lemon juice
¼ teaspoon dried oregano, crumbled
¼ teaspoon freshly ground pepper

Freshly cooked rice

Arrange swordfish in single layer in shallow baking dish. Combine all remaining ingredients except rice in small bowl and mix well. Pour over fish, turning to coat well. Let stand at room temperature, turning once, 30 minutes.

Preheat broiler or prepare barbecue grill. Broil or grill fish 4 inches from heat source for 8 minutes. Baste with sauce, turn and continue cooking until fish flakes easily with fork, about 7 to 10 minutes. Serve over rice.

Swordfish Provençal

The sauce can easily be doubled or tripled, so keep it on hand to serve warm or at room temperature at any time.

2 servings

2 7-ounce swordfish steaks, cut 1 inch thick
1 teaspoon olive oil
Fresh lemon juice to taste
Salt and freshly ground pepper

Provençal Sauce
2 teaspoons olive oil
1 small green bell pepper, seeded and cut into ⅛-inch-thick strips
1 small onion, cut into ⅛-inch-thick slices
½ teaspoon sugar
1 16-ounce can Italian plum tomatoes with basil, drained and coarsely chopped (reserve juice)

2 garlic cloves, flattened
1 continuous strip of peel from 1 small orange
¼ cup anise liqueur
2 teaspoons Herbes de Provence or ½ teaspoon dried lavender, ½ teaspoon dried rosemary, crumbled, and ½ teaspoon fennel seed, crushed
1 teaspoon dried thyme, crumbled
1 teaspoon salt
Freshly ground pepper

Minced fresh parsley (garnish)

Place swordfish in small baking dish. Pat dry, then rub with 1 teaspoon oil, lemon juice, salt and pepper to taste. Set aside at room temperature 1 hour.

For sauce: Heat 2 teaspoons oil in heavy or nonstick large skillet over medium heat. Add pepper and onion. Sprinkle with sugar. Cover partially and cook until vegetables are wilted and just begin to color, about 5 minutes. Add tomatoes, increase heat to high and cook until juices are thickened, about 3 minutes, stirring occasionally. Add reserved tomato juice with garlic and orange peel. Stir in liqueur, Herbes de Provence, thyme, salt and pepper and cook 5 minutes, stirring occasionally. Reduce heat to low, cover partially and simmer until sauce is thickened and vegetables are soft, 30 to 40 minutes. Taste and adjust seasoning. *(Sauce can be prepared 3 days ahead.)*

Grease broiler pan. Preheat broiler. Arrange swordfish on heated pan. Broil fish until juicy inside and charred and crusty outside, turning once and brushing with any juices remaining in baking dish. Transfer to individual plates. Garnish with parsley. Remove orange peel and garlic from sauce. Divide sauce evenly between plates. Serve immediately.

❦ Tuna

Tuna and Watercress Tapenade

This is particularly good spread on lavash or other crisp crackers.

Makes about 2 cups

1 7-ounce can chunk white tuna in oil, drained
½ cup mayonnaise
4 ounces cream cheese, room temperature
2 tablespoons fresh lemon juice
¼ teaspoon freshly ground pepper

2 cups watercress leaves
4 green onions (including green part), trimmed and cut into pieces
3 tablespoons capers
2 tablespoons chopped fresh mint (optional)

Combine tuna, mayonnaise, cream cheese, lemon juice and pepper in processor or blender and blend until smooth. Add watercress, green onion, capers and mint and process using on/off turns until mixture is well blended but retains some texture. Transfer to crock or bowl. Cover mixture and refrigerate for at least 2 hours before serving.

Smoked Albacore Pâté

12 servings

¾ pound smoked albacore,* finely chopped
¾ cup mayonnaise
3 tablespoons chopped yellow onion

3 tablespoons fresh lime juice
⅛ to ¼ teaspoon Worcestershire sauce

Mix all ingredients in processor or blender to puree. Refrigerate pâté until ready to serve.

*Smoked swordfish or dolphinfish can be substituted for smoked albacore.

Portuguese Tuna

Spoon over freshly steamed rice or use to fill warm tortillas.

6 to 8 servings

2 tablespoons oil (or more)
2 onions, chopped
2 garlic cloves, minced
½ cup chopped green bell pepper
¼ cup chopped celery
2 tablespoons chopped fresh parsley
2 8-ounce cans tomato sauce
½ cup water

1 bay leaf
1 3-inch strip orange peel
½ teaspoon cumin
Salt and freshly ground pepper
2 6½-ounce cans tuna, rinsed and drained

Heat 2 tablespoons oil in large skillet over medium-high heat. Add onion, garlic, green pepper, celery and parsley and sauté until tender, about 15 to 20 minutes, adding more oil if necessary. Blend in tomato sauce, water, bay leaf, orange peel, cumin, salt and pepper and bring to boil. Reduce heat and simmer 10 minutes. Add tuna and mix well. Continue simmering 10 minutes. Discard orange peel and bay leaf. Transfer to dish and serve.

❦ *Miscellaneous Saltwater Fish*

Codfish Mousse (Brandade de Morue)

6 to 8 servings

1 pound potatoes, peeled and cut into 1-inch cubes
1 pound fresh cod fillets

¾ cup mayonnaise

1½ to 2 large garlic cloves, crushed
Salt and freshly ground white pepper

Place potatoes in 3- to 4-quart saucepan and lay fish over top. Add water to cover fish completely. Cover and simmer until potatoes are cooked. Pass fish and potatoes through food mill (do not use processor), adding just enough cooking liquid to moisten. Cover and chill.

Combine mayonnaise and garlic in small bowl. Blend into chilled mixture. Season with salt and pepper. (Flavors intensify if mixture is allowed to remain covered in refrigerator several hours.) When ready to serve, taste and adjust seasoning as needed.

Flounder with Shrimp Sauce

2 servings

4 tablespoons (½ stick) butter
2 teaspoons all purpose flour
½ cup milk
3 tablespoons dry Sherry or ¼ cup dry white wine
Salt and freshly ground pepper

6 medium shrimp, shelled, deveined and cut in half
4 large mushrooms, sliced
1 green onion, sliced
2 tablespoons finely chopped parsley
Pinch of dried dillweed

Pinch of paprika
Pinch of dried rosemary, crumbled
Dry Sherry or white wine (optional)

2 teaspoons butter
Juice of ½ lemon
2 flounder fillets (about ¾ pound total)
Freshly cooked rice pilaf

Melt 2 tablespoons butter in heavy small saucepan over low heat. Stir in flour and cook 3 minutes. Add milk and Sherry. Increase heat to medium high and continue cooking, stirring constantly, until sauce boils and is moderately thick. Season with salt and freshly ground pepper. Set aside and keep warm.

Melt 2 tablespoons butter in heavy large skillet over medium-high heat. Add shrimp, mushrooms, green onion, parsley, dillweed, paprika, rosemary, salt and pepper and sauté until shrimp turn pink, about 3 minutes (add Sherry or wine if more liquid is needed). Remove shrimp mixture from skillet and set aside.

Melt remaining 2 teaspoons butter in same skillet over medium heat. Stir in lemon juice. Add flounder and cook until fish turns opaque, about 1 to 2 minutes per side. Season with salt and pepper. Arrange fillets on heated platter. Spoon half of shrimp mixture over fillets. Whisk fish cooking liquid into white sauce and pour over fish. Spoon remaining shrimp over top. Serve immediately with freshly cooked rice pilaf.

Stuffed Flounder

4 servings

4 tablespoons (½ stick) butter, melted
1 2- to 3-pound flounder, boned, or 8 small sole fillets
Salt and freshly ground pepper

Stuffing
4 tablespoons (½ stick) butter
½ cup chopped white onion
½ cup chopped celery
½ cup chopped shallot
¼ cup chopped green bell pepper
1 garlic clove, pressed

1 tablespoon flour
½ cup dry white wine
½ cup milk
½ pound boiled shrimp, chopped
½ pound lump crabmeat, shredded
½ cup breadcrumbs
2 tablespoons chopped fresh parsley
1 egg, lightly beaten
Salt and freshly ground pepper
Ground red pepper

Preheat oven to 375°F. Grease shallow baking pan with 3 tablespoons melted butter. Brush fish with remaining melted butter and season with salt and pepper.

For stuffing: Melt butter in medium skillet over medium-high heat. Add onion, celery, shallot, green pepper and garlic and sauté just until tender. Blend in flour. Add wine and milk and stir until thickened. Remove from heat. Add next 5 ingredients and mix well. Season to taste with salt, pepper and red pepper.

To assemble: Stuff flounder and press edges together to close. If using fillets, divide stuffing over 4, top with remaining fillets and press edges together to seal. Place fish in baking dish, cover and bake 25 minutes. Remove cover and bake 5 minutes longer to brown lightly.

Scrod Fillets with Spinach Cream

4 first-course servings

½ to ¾ pound skinned scrod fillets
Melted butter
Coarse salt
Freshly ground white pepper

Sauce
2 tablespoons (¼ stick) unsalted butter
2 tablespoons minced shallot

5 cups packed spinach leaves, cut into chiffonade (very finely sliced)
⅓ cup dry white wine
1½ cups whipping cream
1 teaspoon Sherry wine vinegar
1 teaspoon coarse salt
Freshly ground white pepper

Preheat oven to 450°F. Remove small bones from fillets with tweezers. Cut fillets on the diagonal, trimming each piece neatly to about 4½ × 2 inches. Lightly brush 4 ovenproof plates with melted butter and sprinkle lightly with salt and pepper. Arrange fish in center of each plate. Brush with butter and sprinkle lightly with salt and pepper. Press small piece of waxed paper on top of fish. Set plates aside.

For sauce: Melt butter in medium skillet over medium heat. Add shallot and cook 1 minute. Add spinach, cover and cook, lifting lid every few seconds to stir, until spinach is completely wilted. Uncover and continue cooking, stirring occasionally, until all liquid is evaporated. Set aside.

Pour wine into small saucepan and cook over medium heat until reduced to 1 tablespoon. Add cream and continue cooking until cream is thickened and reduced to about 1 cup. Stir into spinach. Season with vinegar, salt and a generous amount of pepper.

Bake fish 5 minutes. Remove plates from oven, discard waxed paper and let plates stand 40 seconds. Spoon about ¼ cup sauce around each serving of fish and serve immediately.

Halibut with Saké, Soy Sauce and Ginger (Ni Mono)

8 servings

8 small 1-inch-thick halibut steaks
½ cup mirin* or dry Sherry
½ cup Japanese soy sauce
¼ cup saké or dry Sherry
2 teaspoons sugar
1 teaspoon grated fresh ginger
½ teaspoon salt

8 green onions, green part fringed and spread into fan shape (garnish)
8 paper-thin carrot curls (garnish)

Arrange fish in single layer in large skillet. Combine mirin, soy sauce, saké, sugar, ginger and salt and pour over fish. Cover, place over medium heat and simmer until fish is opaque, about 10 minutes. Transfer to platter. Garnish with green onion fans and carrot curls and serve immediately.

* Available in oriental markets.

Sweet Herring

8 to 10 buffet servings

2 large mild white onions, thinly sliced into rings and separated
Salt

1 16-ounce jar herring pieces in wine sauce

2 large tart apples
1 cup sour cream
1 tablespoon dill seed
1 teaspoon salt

Place onion in colander or sieve; liberally sprinkle with salt. Slowly pour about 1 quart boiling water over top. Rinse well with cold water and let drain. Spread in single layer on paper towels to remove excess moisture.

Drain herring into bowl; discard liquid and onion from jar. Peel, core and dice apples. Add with sour cream, sliced onion, dill and salt to herring and mix gently but thoroughly. Transfer to serving dish.

Curried Herring

8 to 10 buffet servings

1 16-ounce jar herring pieces in wine sauce

1 medium cucumber, peeled, seeded and diced
½ teaspoon salt
1 bunch green onions, chopped

1 mild dill pickle, seeded and diced
1 cup sour cream
2 tablespoons mild curry powder or to taste
1 tablespoon caraway seed

Drain sauce from herring into pan; place herring in mixing bowl. Bring sauce just to boil over medium heat. Immediately pour over herring and let stand 1 minute; drain. Discard onion; cover and chill herring for 1 hour.

Spread cucumber on paper towels. Lightly sprinkle with salt and let stand 15 to 20 minutes. Add to herring with remaining ingredients and mix well.

Sweet and Sour Fish

6 to 8 servings

1½ cups water
1 cup white vinegar
¾ cup sugar
½ teaspoon salt
2 carrots, cut into ¼-inch rounds

2 pounds mackerel or cod steaks, filleted and cut into 1-inch cubes
1 medium onion, sliced into rounds
2 celery stalks, cut into 1-inch pieces

Combine water, vinegar, sugar and salt in large saucepan and bring to boil. Reduce heat, add carrots, cover and simmer until crisp-tender. Add fish and simmer uncovered until opaque. Remove from heat and immediately add onion and celery. Let cool. Marinate overnight in refrigerator, stirring occasionally. When ready to serve, arrange fish and vegetables on platter and pass marinade separately.

Monkfish with Spinach and Béarnaise Sauce (Selle de Lotte)

4 to 6 servings

1 2-pound whole fresh monkfish or sole, skinned (dark meat discarded) and sliced into 4 to 6 fillets ½ inch thick
2 teaspoons chopped fresh tarragon or 1 teaspoon dried, crumbled
¼ teaspoon dried thyme, crumbled
Salt and freshly ground pepper
Olive oil
8 garlic cloves, unpeeled and flattened
1 teaspoon dried chervil, crumbled

2 bunches fresh spinach, stemmed
Salt and freshly ground pepper

¼ cup (½ stick) butter
2 to 3 garlic cloves, peeled and crushed

Béarnaise Sauce
¾ cup white wine vinegar
5 tablespoons finely chopped shallot
Freshly ground pepper
4 egg yolks, beaten
1 cup (2 sticks) butter, melted and clarified
1 teaspoon dried tarragon, crumbled
1 teaspoon dried chervil, crumbled
1 teaspoon minced fresh parsley
¼ teaspoon dried thyme, crumbled
Salt and freshly ground pepper

Olive oil
¼ cup (½ stick) butter

Arrange fillets on platter. Sprinkle with tarragon, thyme, salt and pepper. Drizzle oil over top; sprinkle with unpeeled garlic and chervil. Cover fillets with plastic and chill overnight.

Add half of spinach to large saucepan of boiling salted water. When water returns to boil, immediately remove spinach with slotted spoon and transfer to large bowl of ice water. Drain, squeeze dry and spread out on work surface. Repeat with remaining spinach. Sprinkle with salt and pepper.

Melt butter in large skillet over medium heat. Blend in remaining garlic and cook slowly until butter is light brown (noisette). Remove from heat. Add spinach and toss. Keep warm.

For sauce: Combine vinegar, shallot and pepper in small saucepan over medium-high heat and bring to boil. Let boil until vinegar evaporates and shallot is dry. Transfer 1 tablespoon shallot to metal bowl. Add yolks. Set over *(not in)* hot water over low heat and beat until consistency of mayonnaise. Remove from heat. Add butter one teaspoon at a time, beating constantly. Mix in tarragon, chervil, parsley, thyme, salt and pepper. Taste and adjust seasoning. Cover; keep warm.

SALTWATER FISH • 83

Remove garlic from fish and reserve. Coat bottom of heavy large skillet with olive oil. Place over medium-high heat. Add ¼ cup butter and reserved garlic and sauté until mixture is light brown. Remove garlic from skillet. Add fish fillets and sauté on both sides until lightly browned, about 3 to 4 minutes. Transfer fish to serving platter. Top with sauce and surround with spinach. Serve immediately.

Pompano au Gros Sel, Sauce Noilly

4 to 6 servings

2 pounds coarse salt
2 whole pompano (about 4 pounds each) or 4 to 6 whole trout

1 teaspoon arrowroot
1 cup Noilly Prat dry vermouth

½ cup whipping cream
1¼ cups (2½ sticks) butter, room temperature
Salt and freshly ground pepper

Preheat oven to 400°F. Line baking pans with 2 inches coarse salt. Place fish over top and cover with an additional 2 inches of salt. Bake pompano for 20 minutes.

Meanwhile, combine arrowroot in small bowl with just enough water to make thin paste. Boil vermouth in small saucepan over high heat until reduced to glaze. Add cream, stirring constantly with whisk. Add butter bit by bit, beating constantly until thoroughly mixed. Reduce heat to low, stir in arrowroot and cook until slightly thickened. Add salt and pepper to taste. (Sauce can be made ahead and kept warm over simmering water.)

To serve, remove casing formed during baking and brush all salt from fish. Transfer to platter and discard skin. Fillet into serving pieces and place on heated plates. Spoon sauce to one side.

Mixed Antipasti

Extra virgin Italian olive oil is the special ingredient in this dish, giving added character to the flavors of sardine, eggplant and zucchini.

4 servings

1 8-ounce can boneless sardines in oil, drained and rinsed
¼ cup (about) white wine vinegar
1 large garlic clove, halved

1 small eggplant, thinly sliced crosswise (about 1 pound)
1 teaspoon salt

3 tablespoons olive oil
3 tablespoons fresh lemon juice
1 tablespoon chopped Italian parsley
Freshly ground pepper

¼ cup olive oil
4 small zucchini, thinly sliced on diagonal (about ¾ pound)
1 large garlic clove, halved
3 tablespoons white wine vinegar
4 fresh basil leaves, minced, or ⅛ teaspoon dried, crumbled
1 tablespoon minced Italian parsley

Crusty Italian bread or crisply toasted pita bread

Arrange sardines in single layer in shallow dish. Sprinkle with enough vinegar just to cover. Add 1 garlic clove. Cover dish with plastic wrap and refrigerate at least 24 hours.

Place eggplant in colander. Sprinkle with salt. Set aside to drain 30 minutes.

Preheat broiler. Oil baking sheet. Rinse eggplant and pat dry. Transfer to prepared baking sheet. Broil until tender and easily pierced with knife. Overlap slices on platter. Sprinkle with 3 tablespoons olive oil, then with lemon juice and chopped parsley. Season with pepper. Cover with plastic wrap. Set aside in cool place 24 hours.

Heat ¼ cup oil in large skillet over high heat. Add zucchini and fry until golden, about 6 minutes. Turn mixture into shallow dish. Add garlic, 3 tablespoons vinegar, basil and minced parsley. Cover dish with plastic wrap. Set aside in cool place 24 hours.

To serve, drain all marinades. Arrange sardines, eggplant and zucchini on large platter. Accompany antipasti with Italian bread or pita bread.

Baked Sand Dabs with Grapefruit

2 servings

1 **pound sand dabs or other thin**
   fish fillets
Butter
Juice of 1 grapefruit

1 **tablespoon soy sauce**
1 **tablespoon chopped fresh parsley**
   Freshly cooked rice

Preheat oven to 350°F. Arrange fish in shallow baking dish and dot with butter. Combine grapefruit juice, soy sauce and parsley in small bowl. Pour over fish. Bake until fish is opaque, about 7 to 10 minutes. Serve over rice.

Baked Fish Mozzarella

6 servings

2 **pounds thick flounder or sole**
   fillets
1 **cup shredded mozzarella cheese**
1 **large tomato, thinly sliced**

½ **teaspoon dried oregano**
   Granulated garlic
   Salt and freshly ground pepper

Preheat oven to 375°F. Butter large baking dish. Rinse fillets in salted or acidulated water and pat dry. Arrange in single layer in dish. Sprinkle with cheese and layer with tomato. Dust with oregano, garlic, salt and pepper. Bake until fish is opaque, about 10 minutes. Transfer to heated platter and serve immediately.

4 ❦ *Freshwater Fish*

Freshwater fish are just as plentiful as their oceangoing counterparts. Many of the recipes in this chapter rely on two popular favorites, salmon and trout. Salmon is particularly versatile, in guises from elegant, such as Smoked Salmon Timbales in a sour cream-dill sauce (page 86) or Saumon à la Nage with a tomato-accented Beurre Rouge (page 90) to quick-and-easy entrées like Lomi Lomi Salmon (page 87). There are also delicious recipes from famous restaurants, including Fettuccine with Smoked Salmon (page 92) from the Calistoga Inn in California's Napa Valley.

Trout also lends itself to a variety of presentations. Smoked Trout Mousse with Rye Heart Toast (page 95) is a superb hors d'oeuvre. You can also dress trout up for company in party entrées: Poached Trout with Saffron Butter Sauce (page 98) and Spinach-Stuffed Trout (page 99). Try Green Tortelloni Stuffed with Trout for an Italian flavor.

For a delectable change of pace, select from the remaining freshwater fish presented here, catfish for example. This great Southern favorite, usually fried, is presented here with mango, garlic, ginger, cilantro and chilies for a Southeast Asian dish (page 100).

No matter how you end up preparing a freshwater fish, be sure the fillets selected at the market are shiny with good color—do not buy dull or faded fish. The aroma should be mild and fresh, the meat firm to the touch and not separated from the bones. Any cut surfaces should be moist and not discolored at all. Whenever possible, cook freshwater fish the same day as purchased—or better yet—the same day it was caught.

🍎 *Salmon*

Smoked Salmon Timbales with Sauce

Prepare this appetizer one day before serving for fuller flavor.

8 servings

Sauce
- 6 tablespoons sour cream
- ¼ cup water
- 1 ounce Nova Scotia salmon (lightly salted), finely chopped
- Freshly ground white pepper

Timbales
- 5 ounces Nova Scotia salmon (lightly salted)
- 1 egg white
- 1 tablespoon sour cream
- Freshly ground white pepper
- 1½ teaspoons fresh lemon juice or to taste
- ¾ cup whipping cream
- 1 quart water
- ¾ pound spinach, stems removed
- 2 tablespoons minced fresh dill

For sauce: Mix all ingredients in small bowl. Chill until ready to serve.

For timbales: Combine salmon, egg white, sour cream and white pepper in processor on blender and mix until smooth, about 30 seconds. Transfer to medium bowl. Add lemon juice and additional white pepper to taste. Whip cream in chilled bowl until stiff. Fold into salmon mixture. Cover and refrigerate 2 hours.

Meanwhile, bring water to boil in large saucepan. Add spinach and parboil until just wilted, about 4 *seconds*. Drain well. Run under cold water to stop cooking process. Drain again, squeeze out all remaining moisture. Set aside.

Preheat oven to 325°F. Lightly oil eight ⅓-cup ramekins or dariole molds. Arrange 1 or 2 spinach leaves in bottom of each mold, covering bottom completely. Mince remaining spinach with 1 tablespoon dill. Season lightly with white pepper. Spoon layer of salmon mousse over spinach leaves. Top with minced spinach and cover with remaining mousse. Place ramekins in shallow baking pan. Pour in enough very hot water to come ¾ up sides of molds. Cover each mold with buttered waxed paper and bake for 40 minutes.

Lightly oil baking sheet. Remove ramekins from oven and let stand several minutes. Run edge of knife around each timbale to loosen from mold. Invert onto baking sheet. Cover loosely with lightly oiled waxed paper and chill well, preferably 24 hours.

To serve, center timbales on chilled plates. Spoon about 1½ tablespoons of sauce around each timbale and sprinkle sauce with remaining minced dill.

Fresh Salmon in Saffron and Basil Sabayon

3 to 4 servings

- 1 1-pound salmon fillet
- Olive oil
- Coarse salt
- Freshly ground white pepper

Sabayon
- ¼ cup dry white wine
- Pinch of ground saffron
- 6 egg yolks, lightly beaten
- 3 tablespoons water
- 2 tablespoons (or more) fresh lemon juice
- ½ teaspoon coarse salt
- Freshly ground white pepper
- 2 tablespoons finely chopped fresh basil

Preheat oven to 450°F. If fillet contains a center bone, remove it so there are two fillets. Discard bone and carefully remove any small bones with tweezers. Place fillet skin side down on cutting board and cut fish into ¼-inch slices. Keep slicing until only skin remains to be discarded. Lightly brush 3 or 4 ovenproof plates with olive oil and sprinkle lightly with salt and white pepper. Arrange salmon in center of each plate. Press small piece of waxed paper on top of fish. Set plates aside while preparing sabayon.

For sabayon: Combine wine and saffron in small saucepan and place over low heat just until warmed through. Cool.

Whisk egg yolks in top of double boiler over simmering water until they begin to thicken. Whisk in wine mixture and continue cooking, whisking constantly, until yolks have thickened; *do not overcook or eggs will curdle.* Immediately transfer to mixing bowl and whisk in water. Stir in lemon juice, salt and white pepper. Let sabayon stand at room temperature until ready to use.

Bake salmon 4 minutes. Stir basil into sabayon, adding small amount of water if too thick. Remove plates from oven, discard waxed paper and let plates stand 45 seconds. Spoon about 3 to 4 tablespoons sabayon around each portion to encircle completely and serve.

Lomi Lomi Salmon

In Hawaiian, lomi *means to massage. This dish was originally made with salted salmon, which was "massaged" in water by hand to remove salt.*

2 servings

¼ cup fresh lime juice
2 green onions (including some of green tops), chopped
¼ teaspoon sugar
Pinch of salt
Dash of hot pepper sauce
¼ pound fresh salmon, skinned, boned and cut into small chunks
1 tomato, peeled, seeded and diced

Combine lime juice, onion, sugar, salt and hot pepper sauce in small bowl and mix well. Arrange salmon in another small bowl (do not use metal) and pour marinade over. Cover and refrigerate for at least 6 hours. When ready to serve, shred salmon mixture using fingertips. Add tomato and mix well.

Salmon Mousse

2 servings

1½ teaspoons (½ envelope) unflavored gelatin
3 tablespoons white wine
⅓ pound cooked boned salmon, flaked
⅓ cup mayonnaise
⅓ cup sour cream
1 tablespoon prepared horseradish
1 teaspoon tarragon wine vinegar
1 teaspoon fresh lemon juice
1 teaspoon grated onion
Dash of hot pepper sauce
Dash of Worcestershire sauce
Salt and freshly ground pepper
⅓ cup minced fresh parsley

Lettuce leaves

Dissolve gelatin in white wine in small double boiler or in custard cup in pan with simmering water. Cool. Mix salmon, mayonnaise and sour cream. Stir in cooled gelatin and next 6 ingredients with salt and pepper to taste. Fold in parsley. Rinse 2 small molds with cold water. Divide mousse between molds and chill until firm. To serve, unmold onto bed of lettuce leaves.

Braised Salmon in Lettuce (Filet de Saumon en Laitue)

4 servings

Butter
2 tablespoons dry white wine

8 large shallots, minced
¾ cup white wine vinegar
¾ cup dry white wine
Generous pinch of freshly ground pepper

4 large butter lettuce leaves

1 pound salmon tail, skinned, boned and cut into four 4-ounce fillets
Salt and freshly ground pepper
4 teaspoons butter, room temperature

1 tablespoon chopped fresh chives
Softened butter

3 tablespoons whipping cream
1 tablespoon water
Salt
1½ cups (3 sticks) butter, cut into pieces
Juice of 1 lime
Chopped fresh chives

4 baby carrots, cut julienne, blanched until crisp-tender, drained and sautéed in butter (garnish)

Generously butter baking sheet and sprinkle with 2 tablespoons white wine. Set baking sheet aside.

Combine shallot, vinegar, ¾ cup wine and pepper in medium saucepan and bring to boil over high heat. Continue cooking until liquid evaporates. Transfer shallot to small plate and set aside.

Cut tough ribs from lettuce leaves. Blanch leaves in large saucepan of boiling salted water about 40 seconds. Plunge into cold water to stop cooking process. Drain; dry with paper towels.

Sprinkle fillets on each side with salt and pepper. Set each on lettuce leaf. Dot each with 1 teaspoon butter and sprinkle with chopped chives. Fold leaf over, enclosing fillet completely. Arrange chive side up on prepared sheet. Brush tops with softened butter to prevent drying. Cover with parchment paper and set aside. *Fillets can be prepared ahead to this point. Cover with damp towel instead of parchment paper.*

Preheat oven to 375°F. Combine 2 to 3 tablespoons reserved cooked shallot with cream, water and salt in medium saucepan over medium heat and bring to boil slowly. Gradually whisk in butter. Add additional shallot, if desired. Stir in lime juice and chives to taste.

Bake salmon until just cooked through, about 3 to 4 minutes. Transfer to platter. Top with sauce, garnish with baby carrots and serve.

Saumon Poché Sauce St. Jacques

6 to 8 servings

10 tablespoons (1¼ sticks) unsalted butter
3 shallots, finely chopped
½ pound bay scallops
1 cup dry white wine
Salt and freshly ground pepper
2 cups (1 pint) whipping cream

10 to 15 mushrooms, sliced
¼ pound cooked small shrimp, shelled

2 to 3 cups Court Bouillon (see following recipe)
6 to 8 6-ounce salmon fillets, skinned and boned

Melt 2 tablespoons butter in 10-inch skillet over medium heat. Add shallot and stir until softened. Add scallops, wine, salt and pepper and cook 2 to 3 minutes. Remove scallops from skillet using slotted spoon and set aside. Cook remaining liquid over medium-high heat until reduced by half. Reduce heat to medium, add cream and cook, stirring until sauce is thickened, about 7 to 10 minutes. Whisk in 6 tablespoons butter 1 tablespoon at a time. Remove sauce from heat; set aside and keep warm.

Melt remaining 2 tablespoons butter in large skillet over medium-high heat. Add mushrooms and sauté until cooked and liquid has evaporated, about 5 minutes. Blend into sauce. Slice reserved scallops and add to sauce along with shrimp, mixing well.

Bring court bouillon to simmer in large skillet over high heat. Reduce heat to low, add salmon and poach until cooked through, 6 to 7 minutes (9 minutes per inch of thickness). Drain fillets well. Transfer to warmed plates. Reheat scallop mixture and spoon over fillets. Serve immediately.

Court Bouillon

Makes 3 cups

6 cups water	Bouquet garni (1 bay leaf,
3 small onions, finely chopped	1 parsley sprig, 1 teaspoon dried
3 carrots, finely chopped	thyme, 2 whole peppercorns)
3 celery stalks, finely chopped	1 cup dry white wine
	Salt

Combine water, vegetables and bouquet garni in saucepan and bring to simmer over medium heat. Simmer, uncovered, 20 minutes. Add wine and salt and continue simmering until reduced to 3 cups. Remove court bouillon from heat and strain before using.

Fresh Salmon Slices in Leek Sauce

6 servings

Leek Sauce
- 3 tablespoons butter
- 1½ medium shallots or 1 very large, finely chopped
- 1½ medium tomatoes or 1 very large, peeled, seeded and finely chopped
- ¾ cup fish stock or clam juice
- ¾ cup dry white wine
- 6 tablespoons dry vermouth
- ¾ cup whipping cream
- 1½ large leeks (white part only), thinly sliced

Salmon
- 1½ tablespoons butter (for pan)
- 1½ tablespoons olive oil (for pan)
  Salt and freshly ground white pepper
- 6 salmon steaks about ½ inch thick, boned and skinned (about 1½ to 2 pounds total)

For sauce: Melt 1½ tablespoons butter in large skillet over medium-high heat. Add shallot and sauté just until softened. Add tomatoes and sauté 3 minutes. Remove from heat. Bring stock, wine and vermouth to boil in medium saucepan. Reduce heat and simmer 8 minutes. Stir in cream. Blend into shallot mixture. Cut remaining 1½ tablespoons butter into tiny pieces. Stir sliced leek and butter pieces into sauce.

For salmon: Preheat broiler. Butter and oil baking pan. Sprinkle with salt and pepper to taste. Arrange salmon steaks over. Broil salmon 4 to 6 inches from heat source until just opaque, about 2 minutes on each side. Spoon sauce evenly onto heated plates. Arrange salmon atop sauce. Serve immediately.

Salmon in Basil Sauce (Saumon au Pistou)

If you are unsure about your dishes withstanding broiler heat, use the oven instead. Place rack in upper third and preheat to 450°F. Cook until salmon is just slightly underdone, about two to three minutes. Remember that it will continue cooking from the heat of the sauce. Use very fresh Chinook or King salmon that has not been frozen, cut from the center section of the fish.

4 to 6 servings

1 cup loosely packed fresh basil (without stems)
2 tablespoons (¼ stick) unsalted butter
3 large shallots, sliced
2 medium mushrooms, sliced
2 cups dry white wine
2 cups Fish Fumet (see recipe, page 72)
2 cups whipping cream

8 tablespoons (1 stick) unsalted butter, cut into 4 pieces
Salt (optional)
1 to 2 tablespoons whipping cream

Ovenproof platter, *chilled**
2 pounds boned very fresh salmon, sliced into 1-ounce scallops ¹⁄₁₆ inch thick

Chop ½ cup basil. Melt 2 tablespoons butter in 2-quart saucepan over low heat. Add shallot and mushrooms and cook about 10 minutes. Add wine and chopped basil and cook over medium heat until liquid is reduced by half. Add fumet and cook until liquid is reduced by half. Add cream and continue cooking until sauce is reduced and thickened (it should coat spoon rather heavily).

Strain into another saucepan. Measure about ½ cup of the sauce into blender. Add remaining basil and puree until smooth. Whisk puree into sauce. Place over low heat and finish by whisking in butter 1 piece at a time. Taste and add salt if necessary. Strain and set aside. Keep warm. Just before heating fish stir in 1 to 2 tablespoons cream.

If using broiler, position rack so salmon will be 3 inches from heat source, then preheat. If using oven, position rack in upper third, then preheat to 450°F. Nap bottom of serving platter or plates with sauce. Arrange salmon scallops atop sauce. Broil until top of salmon has changed color and fish is just slightly underdone, about 1 minute.

*Can also be prepared for individual serving using chilled ovenproof or broilerproof dinner plate.

Saumon à la Nage with Beurre Rouge

10 to 12 servings

5 cups dry white wine
5 cups water
6 celery stalks
4 large carrots
2 onions, halved
Bouquet garni (3 large sprigs *each* dill and parsley, 1 bay leaf, pinch of thyme)
Salt and freshly ground pepper

4 red potatoes, peeled and cut into ½-inch slices*
4 large carrots, cut into ½-inch slices*
3 celery stalks, cut into ½-inch slices

1 8-ounce package frozen french-cut green beans, cut into pieces 1½ inches long
1 10-ounce package frozen peas
4 leeks (white part only), cut into ½-inch slices

3 pounds salmon fillets or other firm-fleshed fish

¼ cup minced fresh parsley
2 bunches chives, minced

Beurre Rouge (see following recipe)

Combine first 5 ingredients with bouquet garni in large stockpot and bring to boil. Reduce heat and simmer 30 minutes. Discard vegetables and bouquet garni. Taste and adjust seasoning with salt and pepper if desired. Remove 1 cup stock and transfer to medium saucepan; reserve remaining stock.

Cook each vegetable separately in the 1 cup stock until just crisp-tender. Remove each with slotted spoon before adding next, using the same liquid each time and adding stock as necessary. (Approximate cooking time for each vegetable: 10 minutes for potatoes and carrots, 4 minutes for celery and beans and 3 minutes for peas and leeks.) Set cooked vegetables aside and return remaining liquid to original stock.

Just before serving, bring stock to simmer in large sauté pan or skillet over medium heat. Lower fillets into pan and simmer slowly, allowing 10 minutes cooking time for every inch thickness.

Add vegetables to fish just long enough to heat through. Transfer fillets to large heated platter. Top with vegetables and flavor with some of stock. Sprinkle with parsley and chives. Serve immediately along with beurre rouge.

* For attractive presentation, cut potato slices with crinkle biscuit cutter. Cut carrots with small cookie or canapé cutters.

Beurre Rouge

This sauce cannot be reheated or chilled but will stay warm for 1 hour in wide-neck vacuum bottle rinsed with warm water.

2 **pounds fresh tomatoes, peeled, seeded and chopped (juices reserved)** *	8 **green onions (including some tops), minced**
¼ **cup white wine vinegar**	1 **cup (2 sticks) butter, cut into very small pieces**
¼ **cup dry white wine**	

Combine tomatoes with juices, cover and cook over medium heat 5 minutes. Remove lid and continue cooking until reduced to ½ cup, stirring occasionally to prevent burning or scorching, about 1 hour. Remove from heat and set aside.

In another saucepan, combine vinegar, wine and onion and reduce over medium heat until only 1 tablespoon liquid remains, about 15 minutes. Over *low* heat, gradually whisk in butter 1 piece at a time, blending thoroughly after each is added. Stir in tomato reduction concentrate, blending well.

* If tomatoes are not at their peak of flavor, substitute 2 tablespoons tomato paste.

Salmon Paupiette with Cucumber and Mint

2 to 4 servings

2 **large cucumbers** **Salt**	1 **cup crème fraîche** *or* **whipping cream**
2 **tablespoons (¼ stick) butter**	½ **cup Fish Fumet (see recipe, page 72) or dry white wine**
1 **shallot, minced**	
2 **teaspoons white wine vinegar**	1 **tablespoon butter, melted**
1½ **teaspoons fresh mint, minced, or ½ teaspoon dried mint, crumbled**	**Fresh mint (garnish)**
¼ **teaspoon freshly ground pepper**	
1 **pound fillet of salmon (cut from widest part of salmon), sliced thin and pounded**	

Peel and quarter cucumbers lengthwise. Remove seeds. Cut cucumbers into 1½ × ⅛-inch strips. Sprinkle generously with salt and drain in colander 30 minutes. Rinse thoroughly; drain well.

Heat 1 tablespoon butter in heavy-bottomed skillet over medium heat. Add shallot and stir until translucent. Add cucumbers, vinegar, mint and pepper. Reduce heat to low, cover and cook until cucumbers are tender, stirring occasionally, about 15 minutes.

Transfer ¼ of cucumbers to processor or blender. Add 1 tablespoon butter and puree. Divide among salmon slices. Spread evenly, leaving ½-inch border. Starting with small end, roll up tightly.

Place shallow dish in broiler and preheat. Combine crème fraîche and fumet in small saucepan and boil over high heat until slightly thickened. Pour over remaining cucumbers and mix well.

Cut each paupiette in half. Stand each half *on end* in preheated dish. Drizzle with melted butter. Broil about 3 inches from heat source until paupiettes are just opaque and tops begin to brown, about 5 minutes.

Meanwhile, reheat cucumber. Taste and adjust seasoning. Divide among heated plates. Arrange salmon on top and garnish with sprigs of fresh mint.

Calistoga Inn's Fettuccine with Smoked Salmon

4 main-course or 6 first-course servings

4 cups (1 quart) whipping cream
½ cup (1 stick) butter
¾ pound smoked salmon, cut julienne
¼ cup minced fresh chives

Freshly ground pepper
1 pound freshly cooked fettuccine

Parsley sprigs (garnish)

Combine cream and butter in medium saucepan and cook over medium-high heat until thick, glossy and reduced by half. Add salmon, chives and pepper and cook, stirring gently, about 1 minute. Transfer fettuccine to serving platter. Pour sauce over and toss just to blend. Garnish with parsley and serve.

Smoked Salmon Tart

6 to 8 servings

1 unbaked 9-inch pastry shell
1 egg white, lightly beaten

½ pound smoked salmon,* chopped
1 cup grated Swiss cheese
4 eggs
1¼ cups half and half

1 tablespoon finely snipped fresh dill or 1 teaspoon dried dillweed
½ teaspoon salt
¼ teaspoon freshly ground pepper

Red caviar (optional garnish)

Preheat oven to 400°F. Brush pastry shell lightly with egg white and bake for 5 minutes. Let cool slightly.

Preheat oven to 450°F. Distribute salmon over bottom of pastry and sprinkle with cheese. Beat all remaining ingredients together except garnish and pour over cheese. Bake 15 minutes. Reduce oven temperature to 350°F and continue baking until top is golden, about 15 minutes. Garnish with caviar.

*For economy, use ends and trimmings of smoked salmon, if available.

🍎 *Salmon Trout*

Salmon Trout Soufflé with Sauternes and Ginger

4 servings

3 ounces bay or sea scallops
 Salt and freshly ground pepper
1 egg

3 tablespoons whipping cream

4 boneless salmon trout (about 2 pounds total)

1 tablespoon butter
2 tablespoons minced shallot

½ cup plus 2 tablespoons Sauternes
3 tablespoons dry white wine
¾ cup whipping cream
1 teaspoon grated fresh ginger

 Red rose petals, cut julienne (garnish)
16 cooked asparagus spears (garnish)

Combine scallops, salt and pepper in processor or blender and puree about 30 seconds. Add egg and mix 30 seconds. Transfer mixture (in work bowl with Steel Knife and top intact) to refrigerator and chill for about 30 minutes.

Return work bowl to base. With machine running, pour 3 tablespoons cream through feed tube in slow steady stream and mix 20 to 30 seconds.

Set 1 trout skin side down on work surface. Discard head and fins along sides. Slit trout to separate fillets. Holding tail in left hand, slip knife between skin and flesh and cut in sawing motion with tip of knife to remove skin. Arrange 1 fillet skinned side down on work surface. Using teaspoon, place 4 or 5 dollops of filling lengthwise down fillet. Cut slit in center of remaining fillet, leaving about 1 inch uncut on each end. Lay cut fillet over filling and open slit slightly to allow soufflé to puff through. Repeat with remaining trout.

Spread butter over bottom of large skillet. Sprinkle with shallot. Arrange trout over shallot. Add Sauternes and dry white wine. Season with salt and pepper. Cover, place over high heat and bring to boil. Reduce heat and simmer 2 minutes, shaking pan gently. Set aside, covered, for 1 minute. Transfer trout to dinner plates using slotted spatula. Add cream and ginger to skillet. Place over medium-high heat and cook until sauce is thickened and reduced to about 1 cup. Taste and adjust seasoning. Nap trout with sauce. Garnish with rose petals and asparagus spears. Serve immediately.

Salmon Trout Fillets with Red Wine Sauce
(Filets de Truite Saumonée au Pinot Noir d'Alsace)

6 servings

1¾ pounds shallots
6 salmon trout (3¼ to 3½ pounds total), filleted, backbones and heads reserved
1 750-ml bottle Pinot Noir d'Alsace, Zinfandel or Côtes du Rhône
 Small bouquet garni (1 small parsley sprig, 1 small fresh thyme sprig and 1 bay leaf)
 Salt and freshly ground pepper

16 tablespoons (2 sticks) butter
¾ teaspoon anchovy paste

2 tablespoons all purpose flour
 Green pasta noodles, preferably parsley, but spinach or basil may be substituted

 Chopped fresh parsley (garnish)

Mince 10 medium shallots. Transfer to 2-quart saucepan. Add fish bones and heads, wine, bouquet garni and small dash of salt and pepper. Place mixture over high heat and bring to boil. Reduce heat and simmer 35 minutes, pressing on bones to extract all flavor.

Strain mixture through fine sieve set over bowl. Return liquid to saucepan. Place over medium-high heat and reduce to ¾ cup. Increase heat to high and bring to rapid boil. Add 12 tablespoons butter to center of boil 1 tablespoon at a time, whisking constantly; sauce will be light. Blend in anchovy paste. Taste and season with salt* and ground pepper. Set sauce aside.

Bring large amount of salted water to rapid boil in heavy deep skillet. Add remaining shallots and blanch 3 minutes. Drain well. Pat dry. Melt 2 tablespoons butter in skillet over low heat. Add shallots and cook until tender and golden, stirring occasionally, about 40 minutes. Stir shallots into sauce (shallots will reheat sauce). Add several tablespoons sauce to skillet and stir, scraping up any browned bits. Blend skillet juices back into sauce.

Combine flour, salt and pepper on large plate. Heat 2 tablespoons butter in skillet over medium-high heat. Lightly dredge fillets in flour, patting off excess. Add fillets to skillet and sauté on both sides until just opaque, about 2 minutes on each side. Divide green pasta noodles among individual plates. Top each serving with 2 fillets. Spoon sauce over top. Sprinkle with parsley and serve immediately.

*If sauce is too acidic, add a little more anchovy paste or small amount of concentrated meat extract for seasoning instead of salt.

Smoked Salmon Trout

20 servings

Brine
- 2 large onions, unpeeled, quartered
- 2 large bunches dill or 2 tablespoons dried dillweed
- 2 bunches parsley
- 6 garlic cloves, unpeeled
- 3 large shallots, unpeeled
- 1 4-inch piece ginger, unpeeled
- 1¼ cups soy sauce
- 1 cup red or white wine
- ½ cup liquid brown sugar
- 2 tablespoons coarse salt
- 2 tablespoons onion powder
- 4 whole cloves
- 3 bay leaves
- 1 teaspoon garlic powder
- ¼ teaspoon mace

- 1 10- to 12-pound salmon trout*
- 5 pounds hickory or other wood chips

  Charcoal briquets

  Vegetable oil pan spray

Garnish
- 2 heads Bibb lettuce
- 2 large onions
- 3 eggs
- ¾ cup capers, drained
- 3 lemons, cut into thin wedges
  Horseradish Sauce (see following recipe)

For brine: Combine onion, dill, parsley, garlic, shallots and ginger in processor or blender and puree. Turn into glass or enamel dish just large enough to hold fish. Add remaining ingredients and mix well. Add enough cold water (about 2 cups) to raise depth of brine 3 inches, and stir thoroughly. Add fish and just enough water to cover. Refrigerate 2 to 3 days, turning several times.

Soak hickory chips overnight in water.

To smoke: Prepare barbecue by heaping briquets *on one side* of grill (start with about 30 for large grill). Ignite and burn until coals glow and gray ash forms.

Set drip pan opposite briquets. Remove fish from brine and wipe dry.

Pile hickory chips over briquets. Set top grill in place and coat side over drip pan with vegetable oil pan spray. Immediately set fish over drip pan and tightly cover barbecue. Leave one or two vents open to allow smoke to escape. Smoke until fish flakes when tested with fork, allowing about 8 minutes per pound. *(Time will depend on weather; if temperature is quite cold, it can take up to two hours or even longer.)* Add coals as necessary if briquets begin to burn down.

Transfer fish to large platter and let cool. Cover and refrigerate until 1 hour before ready to serve.

For garnish, separate lettuce leaves carefully, using only those that form a perfect cup. Chop onions and place in paper towel-lined sieve to dry slightly.

Place eggs in saucepan and cover with cold water. Bring to boil and let boil 1 minute. Turn off heat and let stand 5 minutes. Cool under cold running water. Peel, chop and set aside.

To serve, surround fish with lettuce cups alternately filled with onion, egg, capers and lemon wedges. Pass Horseradish Sauce separately.

*Ten 8- to 10-ounce trout can be substituted for the large fish. Allow 1 day in brine and 45 to 60 minutes for smoking.

Horseradish Sauce

3 tablespoons finely chopped fresh dill or 1 tablespoon dried dillweed
1 tablespoon green peppercorns, drained and crushed
1 teaspoon onion powder
Dash of ground red pepper

Dash of mace
2 cups (1 pint) sour cream
½ cup grated fresh horseradish or drained horseradish in vinegar, or more to taste

Paprika (garnish)

Combine dill, peppercorns, onion powder, red pepper and mace in bowl and mix well. Add sour cream and stir lightly. Blend in horseradish *(do not beat or sour cream will thin)*. Transfer to sauceboat, cover and refrigerate. Sprinkle with paprika and serve chilled.

 *Trout*

Smoked Trout Mousse with Rye Heart Toast

Makes 2 to 2½ cups

1 pound smoked trout, skinned and boned
½ cup sliced green onion
¼ to ⅓ cup loosely packed fresh dill or 1 teaspoon dried dillweed
2 tablespoons plus 2 teaspoons fresh lemon juice
¼ teaspoon freshly ground pepper

1 cup whipping cream
Salt (optional) and freshly ground pepper
Additional fresh lemon juice

1 fresh dill sprig (garnish)
Rye Heart Toast (see following recipe) or crisp crackers

Combine trout, green onion, dill, lemon juice and ¼ teaspoon pepper in processor or blender and chop finely using 5 to 6 on/off turns. With machine running, slowly pour cream through feed tube and blend well. Taste and adjust seasoning with salt, pepper and lemon juice. Transfer to crock or serving bowl. Cover with plastic wrap. Chill mousse several hours or overnight. Garnish with fresh dill sprig. Serve with Rye Heart Toast or crackers.

Rye Heart Toast

1 1-pound loaf very thinly
   sliced rye bread

Preheat oven to 375°F. Using 2-inch heart-shaped cookie cutter, cut out as many hearts as desired from bread (reserve trimmings to make crumbs for another use). Arrange hearts in single layer on ungreased baking sheets. Bake, turning once, until crisp and lightly colored, about 4 to 6 minutes per side. Transfer to rack and cool before serving.

Green Tortelloni Stuffed with Trout
(Tortelloni Verdi di Trota)

This stuffed pasta, shaped like a pointed hat, is a larger version of tortellini.

4 servings

Trout Filling
3 to 4 tablespoons butter
2 medium whole trout (about ¾ pound total), slit ½ inch deep along backbone

½ cup dry white wine
   Juice of 1 lemon
3 to 4 tablespoons whipping cream
1 tablespoon minced fresh parsley
   Salt and freshly ground pepper

Tortelloni
1 pound fresh spinach, stemmed (about 1 large bunch), or 1 10-ounce package frozen spinach
1 cup water
1 teaspoon salt

2 cups all purpose flour (preferably unbleached)
3 eggs, room temperature

Fresh Tomato Sauce
¼ cup olive oil
⅓ small hot red or green chili
1 large garlic clove, minced
2 pounds tomatoes, peeled, cored, seeded and finely diced
⅓ cup whipping cream
2 teaspoons chopped fresh basil
1 teaspoon minced fresh parsley
1 teaspoon minced fresh oregano

   Butter

For filling: Melt butter in heavy large skillet over medium-high heat. Reduce heat to medium low, add trout and cook 4 minutes. Turn trout over and cook until done, about 3 more minutes (or about 9 minutes total per inch of thickness). Using sharp thin knife, remove skin and then lift off fillet. Carefully lift off bone, removing any tiny bones with strawberry huller or tweezers. Turn trout over and remove skin from remaining fillet. Cut trout into chunks. Repeat with other fish.

Pour wine into same skillet. Place over medium-high heat and cook until wine is reduced to 1 tablespoon. Stir in lemon juice and cook until reduced to 1 tablespoon. Add cream and parsley, blending well. Season with salt and pepper. Stir in trout. Transfer mixture to processor or blender and mix using on/off turns just until trout is finely chopped; *do not puree.* Pour filling into bowl. Chill at least 1 hour to firm.

For tortelloni: Combine spinach, water and salt in large pot or Dutch oven over high heat. Cover and bring to boil. Cook until spinach is tender, about 2 to 3 minutes (if using frozen spinach, cook according to package directions). Drain spinach and squeeze dry; mince finely. Arrange flour in mound on work surface and make well in center. Break eggs into well and beat eggs lightly with fork until blended. Stir cooked spinach into eggs.

Gather dough into loose mass and set aside. Scrape any hard bits of flour from work surface and discard. Lightly flour work surface and hands. Knead dough until smooth and elastic, 10 to 12 minutes. Insert finger in center of dough; if dry, dough is ready for pasta machine; if sticky, sprinkle dough lightly with

🐚 *Microwave Tips and Techniques for Fish*

Fish is one of the foods the microwave does best. The speedy cooking brings out the light, fresh taste of seafood in no time. The most important thing to remember is that most fish is delicate and overcooking can happen quickly in a microwave. To avoid this, always use the minimum time suggested in the recipe and then test for doneness. The moment fish turns opaque it is done; cooking it longer will make it dry and chewy. So if you are preparing fish ahead to serve later, undercook slightly and reheat on High to desired doneness just before serving time.

A word about frozen fish. Defrost at about 30 percent power for a minimum of time. As soon as the pieces can be separated, turn the power off and let the fish stand until it is completely thawed. Refrigerate until ready to use, but try to cook it soon after defrosting.

Poaching
For best results when poaching seafood, always arrange it with the thickest portion facing the rim of the dish and the thinner portions toward the center. Cover loosely with waxed paper to promote even cooking. As a general guide, allow four minutes per pound for thick fish steaks and two to three minutes per pound for thinner cuts. If the fish is quite thin, such as sole and other fillets, there is no need to turn it during cooking. Just let it stand in the hot liquid with the power off to finish. Vary the poaching liquid to enhance flavor: use white wine, clam juice, chicken broth or tomato juice.

Using Plain or Herbed Coatings
Fish fillets or steaks coated with breadcrumbs, crushed cornflakes or other similar mixtures should not be covered with airtight wrapping. Cover with a paper towel instead.

Grilling
A browning dish is ideal for grilling in the microwave, especially for thick cuts of fish such as halibut or salmon steaks. Cover loosely with waxed paper when cooking. For maximum surface crisping, always turn fish over as soon as juices begin to appear on top.

Steaming
Cover dish tightly with plastic wrap to promote as much moisture as possible.

flour and continue kneading until dough is correct consistency. To knead and shape dough in pasta machine, cut off 1 egg-size piece of dough. Store remaining dough in plastic wrap or dry towel to prevent drying; set aside. Flatten piece of dough with heel of hand, then fold in half. Turn pasta machine to widest setting and run dough through. Continue folding and kneading with pasta machine until dough is smooth and velvety, about 2 more times (depending on how vigorously dough was kneaded by hand). Dust lightly with more flour as necessary.

Adjust pasta machine to next narrower setting. Run dough through machine *without folding,* dusting lightly with flour if sticky. Repeat, narrowing rollers after each run until machine is on second to narrowest setting; pasta should be less than ¹⁄₁₆ inch thick.

To shape tortelloni, immediately cut 1 dough sheet into 3-inch squares. Place 1 heaping teaspoon filling in center of 1 square. Fold pasta square in half diagonally to form triangle, pressing edges to seal. Bend triangle around finger, pressing 1 pointed end over other end to seal. Transfer to kitchen towel set on baking sheet, spacing evenly. Repeat with remaining dough. *(Tortelloni can be prepared ahead to this point. Cover with kitchen towel and refrigerate until ready to cook.)*

For sauce: Heat oil in heavy saucepan over medium heat. Add hot chili and garlic and sauté 2 minutes. Add tomatoes. Bring mixture slowly to boil and cook until tomato liquid has evaporated and mixture is thickened, about 12 minutes (length of cooking time will depend on juiciness of tomatoes). Stir in cream, basil, parsley and oregano and continue cooking until reduced to saucelike consistency.

To cook pasta, fill pasta cooker or stockpot ¾ full with salted water and bring to rapid boil over high heat. Stir in 1 tablespoon oil. Add pasta and stir vigorously to prevent sticking. Cook until just firm but tender to bite (al dente), about 5 to 20 seconds for freshly made pasta and up to 3 minutes for that which has thoroughly dried. Taste often to prevent overcooking. Drain.

Butter heated serving platter. Transfer pasta to platter. Add sauce and toss gently until pasta is well coated. Serve hot.

Poached Trout with Saffron Butter Sauce

This dish can also be made with a larger trout or steelhead to serve several people. The method and dramatic presentation are still the same.

2 servings

2 8-ounce trout, cleaned
2 to 3 cups Court Bouillon (see following recipe)

1 teaspoon saffron threads dissolved in about 2 tablespoons dry white wine

2 cups (about 8 medium) tomatoes, peeled, seeded, squeezed dry and chopped
8 tablespoons (1 stick) unsalted butter
Salt and freshly ground pepper

Italian parsley leaves (garnish)

Poach trout in just enough court bouillon to cover until done (trout should be soft to the touch and pinkness around backbone should just disappear). Lift out carefully and let drain; keep warm.

Strain liquid; return half to sauté pan and boil until reduced by ⅔. Add saffron and reduce another few minutes.

Place trout on hot plates and peel off skin. Warm tomatoes in another sauté pan with 2 tablespoons of the butter, ¼ cup reserved court bouillon, and salt and pepper to taste. Reheat saffron sauce, add remaining butter in pieces and stir until thoroughly melted and combined. Surround fish with tomatoes, then pour sauce around fish. Float a few parsley leaves in the sauce.

Court Bouillon

Makes 2 to 3 cups

6 cups water
3 small onions, finely chopped
3 carrots, finely chopped
3 celery stalks, finely chopped
Bouquet garni (1 bay leaf, 1 parsley sprig, 1 teaspoon dried thyme, 2 whole peppercorns)

1 cup dry white wine
Salt

Combine water, vegetables and bouquet garni in saucepan and simmer uncovered 20 minutes. Add wine and salt and continue simmering 20 minutes. Strain.

Spinach-Stuffed Trout

2 servings

6 tablespoons (¾ stick) unsalted butter
2 shallots, finely minced
½ cup sliced mushrooms
½ bunch (6 to 7 ounces) fresh spinach, coarsely chopped
4 tablespoons minced fresh parsley
¼ teaspoon dried tarragon, crumbled

Salt and freshly ground pepper
2 small trout (about ½ pound each), boned

2 tablespoons fresh orange juice
½ teaspoon fresh lemon juice

Orange slices (garnish)

Melt 2 tablespoons butter in medium skillet over high heat. Add shallots and mushrooms and sauté briefly. Add spinach, 2 tablespoons minced parsley and tarragon. Reduce heat and cook, stirring constantly, until most of moisture has evaporated. Sprinkle with salt and pepper to taste. Stuff each trout with half of spinach mixture.

Melt remaining 4 tablespoons butter in another medium skillet over medium heat. Add trout and sauté until golden brown, about 5 minutes per side. Transfer to heated platter and keep warm.

Add orange juice to skillet. Stir in lemon juice and remaining parsley. Cook over high heat, stirring constantly, until sauce is slightly thickened. Pour over fish. Garnish and serve.

🍒 *Miscellaneous Freshwater Fish*

Fish with Coriander Sauce

6 to 8 servings

3 tablespoons oil
2 large onions, thinly sliced
1 tablespoon minced fresh garlic
4 cups peeled, diced tomatoes
1 small hot red chili pepper, chopped, or ¼ teaspoon ground red pepper
3 tablespoons minced fresh coriander (also known as cilantro or Chinese parsley)
1 tablespoon dried coriander

1 tablespoon cumin
1 bay leaf
Salt and freshly ground pepper
2 to 2½ pounds whitefish fillets or steaks, freshly baked or poached and kept warm

Lime wedges and hard-cooked eggs, quartered (garnish)

Heat oil in large saucepan over medium-high heat. Add onion and sauté until softened. Add garlic and continue cooking 1 minute. Add remaining ingredients except fish and garnishes and bring to boil. Reduce heat and simmer, uncovered, 10 to 15 minutes. Pour over fish and surround with garnish of lime wedges and hard-cooked egg quarters.

🍒

Dalmatian Fish Stew

6 to 8 servings

2 tablespoons olive oil
1 cup thinly sliced onion
2½ pounds skinned whitefish fillets, cut into squares
¾ cup dry red wine
½ cup wine vinegar

3 tablespoons tomato paste
Dash of dried basil leaves
Salt and freshly ground pepper

Chopped fresh parsley
Freshly cooked rice

Heat oil in large skillet over medium heat. Add ½ cup onion and sauté until translucent. Arrange fish squares in single layer over onion. Distribute remaining ½ cup onion over top. Sauté, turning once, until fish begins to brown. Combine wine, vinegar, tomato paste, basil, salt and pepper and pour over fish. Cover and simmer about 1 hour, gently shaking pan occasionally and adding additional wine or water if necessary (you will want a fair amount of liquid with this dish). Sprinkle with parsley and serve with rice.

Dalmatian Fish Stew can be reheated.

Crisp-Fried Catfish (Yam Pla Dook)

4 to 6 servings

2 pounds catfish fillets

3 cups vegetable oil (for deep frying)

1 unripe (green) mango, peeled, seeded and shredded*

8 medium garlic cloves, thinly sliced and fried in 1 tablespoon vegetable oil until crisp

1 3-inch piece fresh ginger, minced or finely shredded

2 tablespoons sugar
2 tablespoons fish sauce (nam pla)**
Juice of 2 limes (about 2 tablespoons)

2 red serrano chilies, seeded and slivered (garnish)
1 tablespoon fresh cilantro leaves (also known as coriander or Chinese parsley) (garnish)

Fit large saucepan with steamer rack. Add water to just below rack. Bring to rapid boil over high heat. Add fish fillets and steam until opaque and just tender, about 8 to 10 minutes. Let cool.

Heat oil in wok to 375°F. Pat fish dry. Remove any bones. Cut fish into bite-size pieces. Add fish to wok in batches and fry until crisp and well browned. Remove catfish with slotted spoon and drain thoroughly on paper towels.

Mix mango, garlic and ginger in small bowl. Mound in center of serving platter. Surround with fried fish. Combine sugar, fish sauce and lime juice in cup and stir until sugar dissolves. Sprinkle most of sauce over mango mixture. Sprinkle remaining sauce over fish. Garnish with chilies and cilantro. Serve immediately.

*Hard, semiripe peaches can be substituted.
**Available in Asian markets.

5 ❦ Basic and Mixed Dishes

Mixed seafood dishes present a delightful opportunity for the innovative cook. The combinations are virtually unlimited. Mingling different types and textures of seafood in the same dish gives unique palate-pleasing results.

The recipes in this chapter are undeniably delicious—but they are also guidelines for inspiring your own ideas. Several of them, such as Whole Baked Fish, Dalmation Style (page 111) or Fish Timbales with Oyster Sauce (page 102) are basic recipes that let you choose the foundation of the dish from a variety of fish—a big help considering that the selection at the market can vary from day to day.

Other dishes use several kinds of fish to delectable advantage. For instance, Boudins de Fruits de Mer (page 110) are fabulous shellfish sausages of pureed sole with bits of shrimp and scallops in a sauce made with fresh oysters. It is a superb party appetizer or entrée for a fancy luncheon. Marseilles-Style Grilled Skewers of Shrimp, Scallop and Squid (page 109) are delightful additions to a menu for outdoor entertaining. For an ethnic flavor, try Tempura (page 106), Risotto con Frutti di Mare (page 108) or Pasta Primavera Salad with Seafood and Basil Cream (page 107).

No matter what the occasion—a special dinner party, Sunday supper for the family or just a midweek change of pace dish to keep meals interesting, you will find that these basic ideas and mixed seafood dishes are easy on the cook, pleasing to the eye and irresistible to the palate.

Fish Timbales with Oyster Sauce

A dry white wine such as Chardonnay or Chablis would enhance this rich and glamorous first course.

6 servings

½ pound fish fillets (sole, pike or turbot)
2 cups milk
4 egg yolks
2 eggs
1 teaspoon dried dillweed
1 teaspoon salt

¼ teaspoon freshly ground white pepper

Oyster Sauce (see following recipe)

Minced fresh parsley (garnish)

Preheat oven to 350°F. Generously butter six ½-cup molds or ovenproof cups. Puree fish until smooth in processor or blender. Add milk, yolks, eggs, dill, salt and pepper and mix until creamy. Divide evenly among prepared molds.

Cover each mold with round of buttered waxed paper and set into large pan. Add enough boiling water to come halfway up sides of molds. Bake until set, about 30 minutes. Remove molds from water and let stand 5 minutes. Discard waxed paper. Unmold timbales onto warm plates or serving platter by running tip of sharp thin knife around inside edge of mold. Spoon some of Oyster Sauce over each timbale and sprinkle with parsley. Serve immediately accompanied with remaining sauce.

Oyster Sauce

Makes 3 cups

1 cup fresh oysters, undrained

2 cups crème fraîche
1 teaspoon fresh lemon juice or to taste

Salt and freshly ground pepper
3 tablespoons minced fresh parsley

Poach oysters in their liquor in small saucepan until firm. Drain well. Chop oysters finely and set aside.

Bring crème fraîche just to boil over medium heat. Reduce heat and simmer gently until crème fraîche has thickened and lightly coats spoon, about 20 minutes. Blend in lemon juice, salt and pepper. Stir in oysters and parsley.

Shrimp, Scallop and Sole Mousse

8 to 10 buffet servings

⅓ cup oil (¾ vegetable oil and ¼ olive oil)
½ pound uncooked large shrimp, shelled, deveined and cut into quarters
½ pound sea scallops, cut into quarters
1½ cups chicken stock
1 tablespoon fresh lemon juice
4 sprigs Italian parsley
2 bay leaves

¼ teaspoon dried tarragon leaves
¼ teaspoon dried whole thyme
½ pound skinned and boned sole or flounder fillets, cut into strips

1½ tablespoons (1½ envelopes) unflavored gelatin
¼ cup dry vermouth
1 teaspoon salt
¼ teaspoon freshly ground pepper

4 eggs, separated and brought to room temperature

Heat oil in deep large skillet until very hot but not discolored. Add shrimp and scallops and stir constantly until just barely cooked through, 1 to 1½ minutes. Remove from heat and drain well, reserving oil. Set shrimp and scallops aside to cool completely.

Combine stock, lemon juice, parsley, bay leaves, tarragon and thyme in saucepan and bring to boil. Add fish fillets and simmer for 5 minutes.

Meanwhile, chop shrimp and scallops into very fine pieces, *but do not mince.*

Sprinkle gelatin over vermouth to soften. Remove bay leaves from stock and transfer hot mixture to blender. Add dissolved gelatin, salt and pepper and blend on high speed until uniformly pureed, about 1 minute.

Return to saucepan and bring to boil. Add reserved oil. Remove from heat and beat in egg yolks one at a time. Pour into bowl and chill well, stirring occasionally until mixture is very thick and almost set, about 1 hour. Stir in chopped shrimp and scallops.

Lightly oil 7- or 8-cup mold. Beat egg whites until stiff but not dry. Fold ⅓ into chilled seafood mixture to lighten, then fold in remainder, blending gently but completely. Turn into mold, tapping on counter to remove any air bubbles. Cover; chill until set, at least 6 hours. Unmold onto chilled plate.

Fish Balls with Snow Peas and Asparagus

The chef at The Mandarin restaurant in San Francisco prepares these fish balls by hand, beginning with two cleavers to chop the fish very finely. His techniques cannot be readily described since he has a "sixth sense" about the feel of the paste. A processor, however, makes preparation much easier and comes closest to duplicating the chef's expertise. If you do prepare this recipe without a processor, the fish will require at least 15 minutes of chopping and kneading.

6 to 8 servings

1½ pounds finely chopped rock cod, sea bass or white fish fillets
1 tablespoon dry Sherry
1 tablespoon dark sesame oil*
3 large egg whites
    Few drops freshly squeezed ginger root juice**
    Few drops freshly squeezed green onion juice (white part only)**
1 teaspoon salt

¼ cup peanut oil
    Pinch of salt

¼ pound snow peas
3 to 4 stalks diagonally sliced asparagus
½ cup bamboo shoots

    Dark sesame oil
¾ cup Virginia ham, cut julienne

1 medium tomato (garnish)

    Soy sauce

Using double Steel Blade in work bowl combine fish, Sherry, oil, 1 egg white, ginger and onion juices, and salt. Process 2 minutes, stopping frequently to stir. Add remaining egg whites 1 at a time in the same manner (mixture will be smooth and gelatinous). Transfer to medium bowl and stir with spatula to break up mixture slightly.

Fill a wok half full with water. Bring to boil over high heat. Turn off heat. Wet hands with cold water. With one hand squeeze a portion of fish mixture through hollow between thumb and base of index finger to form ball. Scoop up mass with spoon dipped in water. (This method requires practice; you may find it easier to form balls with your fingers or a tablespoon.)

Place each ball in wok (they will sink to bottom). As they begin to float to surface, about 2 minutes, turn up heat and boil gently 5 to 6 minutes. Remove with wire strainer or slotted spoon and place in bowl of cold water. *This may be done 1 day ahead.*

Heat wok or frying pan until very hot. Add a small amount of peanut oil and salt. *Individually* stir-fry snow peas, asparagus and bamboo shoots briefly, about 2 to 3 minutes, adding more oil with each vegetable. Arrange asparagus spoke-fashion on heated serving platter. Top with snow peas.

Add remaining peanut oil and stir-fry fish balls 1 minute. Sprinkle sesame seed oil sparingly over top. Mound fish balls in center and top with bamboo shoots and ham. Garnish with tomato wedges and serve immediately. Pass soy sauce separately in small bowl or pitcher.

*Available in oriental markets.

**Use garlic press to squeeze ginger and onion juices.

🍎 *Classic Sauces for Fish*

Blender Bearnaise Sauce

Makes 1½ cups

2 tablespoons tarragon vinegar	¼ teaspoon salt
2 teaspoons fresh tarragon or 1 teaspoon dried tarragon	¼ teaspoon mustard
6 shallots, minced	⅛ teaspoon meat glaze (Bovril)
2 tablespoons dry white wine	⅛ teaspoon Sauce Robert*
4 egg yolks	1 cup (2 sticks) butter, melted

In small pan, heat tarragon vinegar, tarragon, shallots and wine, and simmer until almost all liquid is absorbed.

Place mixture in blender and add egg yolks, salt, mustard, meat glaze, and Sauce Robert. Blend for 15 seconds.

Heat butter until sizzling hot. Immediately pour hot butter in a steady stream into the running blender. Blend until thick.

*Escoffier's Sauce Robert is available at fine food stores.

If you place béarnaise sauce immediately into a preheated thermos, it will hold perfectly for 1 hour. This works for hollandaise too.

Green Mayonnaise (Sauce Verte)

Makes 2 cups

1 cup loosely packed spinach leaves, cleaned and thoroughly dried, stems removed	¼ teaspoon dry mustard
3 sprigs fresh parsley	1 teaspoon basil *or* tarragon
¼ cup watercress, leaves only	2 anchovy fillets
2 tablespoons lemon juice	1 cup mayonnaise
2 tablespoons chopped green onion	2 tablespoons capers, drained and rinsed

Place all ingredients except capers in a blender or processor and mix for 10 to 15 seconds.

Transfer to a bowl and fold in capers. Refrigerate. Serve with shellfish, halibut, striped bass, swordfish or trout.

Mustard Dill Sauce

Makes 2½ cups

½ cup sugar	⅓ cup wine vinegar
1 cup fresh dill	½ cup mayonnaise
1 cup Dijon mustard	2 tablespoons oil

Combine all ingredients except oil in a blender or processor. Blend until mixture is smooth.

While blender is still running, add oil, drop by drop, until absorbed. Store covered in refrigerator. Serve with salmon or shrimp.

Sauce Tartare

Makes 1¼ cups

1 cup mayonnaise	1 tablespoon finely chopped fresh chervil
1 tablespoon finely chopped fresh parsley	1 tablespoon capers, drained and rinsed
1 tablespoon finely chopped chives	1 small sour pickle, chopped
1 tablespoon finely chopped fresh tarragon	3 lemons, halved and hollowed

Combine all ingredients and use to fill hollowed lemon halves. Serve with scallops or grilled fish.

Sauce Rémoulade

Makes 2 cups

1½ cups mayonnaise	2 tablespoons chopped fresh tarragon leaves *or* fresh chervil
1 generous teaspoon Dijon mustard	1 anchovy fillet
2 tablespoons chopped gherkin	
2 tablespoons capers, drained and rinsed	
2 tablespoons chopped fresh parsley	

Combine all ingredients in blender or processor. Blend until smooth. Allow to mellow in refrigerator for at least 3 hours. Serve with shellfish, fish steaks or any grilled white fish.

Parsley Butter

Makes 1 cup

1 cup (2 sticks) butter	Freshly ground black pepper
¼ cup minced fresh parsley	
2 tablespoons lemon juice or to taste	

Cream butter and add remaining ingredients. Mix thoroughly. Use for basting and as a sauce with whole grilled fish.

Hilton Harbour Castle Poissons Crus Marinés

1 serving

2 ounces uncooked fresh fish, thinly sliced (1 ounce each of 2 different fish, such as salmon, tuna and red snapper)
1 ounce bay or sea scallops, sliced
1½ teaspoons white wine
Juice of ½ small lemon
½ teaspoon minced red pickled ginger*
Thinly sliced green onion

Dash of Japanese fragrant pepper (sansho)*

1 small Boston lettuce leaf
2 teaspoons red salmon caviar
1 small artichoke heart, cooked and chilled

1 lemon wedge, seeded (garnish)
2 thin slices rye bread, buttered

Arrange fish and scallop slices at one side of chilled salad plate. Combine wine and lemon juice and pour over fish. Sprinkle with pickled ginger. Let stand 3 minutes (lemon juice will "cook" fish). Sprinkle dish with sliced green onion and Japanese fragrant pepper.

Lay lettuce leaf along other side of plate. Spoon caviar into artichoke heart and set atop lettuce. Garnish with lemon wedge and bread and serve.

*Available in oriental markets.

Tempura

8 servings

Seafood (choose among the following)
   Whole clams, scallops, mussels or oysters, shelled
   Shrimp or prawns, shelled and deveined
   Whole small fish, cleaned
   Fillet of fish cut into strips

   Oil for deep frying (preferably peanut oil)

Vegetables (choose several of the following)
   Mushrooms (sliced if large, whole if small)
   Spinach leaves
   Snow peas or sugar snap peas, strings removed
   Sweet potatoes, peeled and cut into thin slices
   Carrots, peeled and cut into thin diagonal slices

   Eggplant, peeled and cut into ¼-inch julienne
   Watercress or parsley sprigs
   Green beans, blanched 5 minutes in boiling water, drained, rinsed in cold water and well drained
   Green onions, cut into 2-inch diagonal slices
   Zucchini, cut into ¼-inch julienne

Dipping Sauce
   1 cup Dashi (see following recipe) or light chicken or fish stock
   ¼ cup Japanese soy sauce
   ¼ cup mirin* or dry Sherry
   1 tablespoon grated white turnip
   ½ teaspoon grated fresh ginger

Batter
   3 eggs
   ⅔ cup ice water
   1 cup all purpose flour

Arrange seafood and vegetables on large platter.

Preheat oil in wok, deep fryer or electric skillet to 375°F.

For sauce: Combine all ingredients and blend well. Divide evenly among small individual serving bowls.

For batter: Combine eggs and ice water in bowl and beat well. Sift in flour, whisking until well blended (batter should be thin and run easily off spoon; if too thick, thin with a little additional ice water). Do not let batter stand any longer than 10 minutes.

To cook tempura: Dip each piece of food into batter, coating well. Add to oil in batches of 6 to 8 pieces. Cook 1 minute, then turn each piece with tongs or chopsticks and continue frying until evenly golden, about 1 more minute.

Drain well on paper towels. Serve immediately. *(Can be kept warm in 250°F oven about 5 minutes without losing crispness. If prepared at table in electric skillet or deep fryer, serve each piece as it is cooked.)*

To create tempura "pine needle" garnish, break thin uncooked somen *noodles (also known as Chinese vermicelli) into 3-inch lengths. Gather into bundles about ⅓ inch in diameter. Dip ½ inch of one end into tempura batter. Holding bundle tightly, dip batter-coated end in hot oil and fry 30 seconds to seal. Carefully let go of bundle, allowing noodles to fall into oil and fan out. Continue frying until noodles just turn brown. Drain on paper towels.*

* Available in oriental markets.

Dashi

This clear, light stock, traditionally used as a soup base, gives Japanese food its distinctive flavor.

Makes about 4 cups

4 cups water
1 sheet dried black seaweed
   (yamadashi)

½ cup dried bonito flakes

Combine water and seaweed in large saucepan and bring to boil over high heat. Reduce heat to medium low and simmer 5 minutes. Remove from heat. Discard seaweed. Blend in bonito flakes. Let stand until flakes sink to bottom of saucepan. Strain mixture into airtight storage container.

Pasta Primavera Salad with Seafood and Basil Cream

This one-dish meal makes a spectacular buffet centerpiece. To allow flavors to mellow, Pasta Primavera should be prepared one to three days ahead.

12 to 16 buffet servings or 8 to 10 main-course servings

Pasta (prepare 1 to 3 days ahead)
1 pound Italian fettuccine, broken into 2-inch pieces
   Salt
⅓ cup light olive oil
¼ cup white wine vinegar
1 tablespoon Spanish Sherry wine vinegar
   Salt and freshly ground pepper

Vegetables (prepare 1 to 2 days ahead)
16 very thin asparagus spears, trimmed of tough ends, cut into 1½-inch lengths
2 to 3 cups broccoli florets cut into bite-size pieces
2 to 3 cups fresh peas or frozen tiny peas, defrosted

6 green onions

1 pint small cherry tomatoes
1 pound fresh young spinach leaves

Seafood (prepare no more than 1 day ahead)
2 pounds bay or sea scallops
2 pounds uncooked large shrimp
⅓ cup olive oil
3 tablespoons wine vinegar
3 tablespoons Spanish Sherry wine vinegar
1 garlic clove, minced

2 green onions, minced
   Salt and freshly ground pepper
   Basil Cream (see following recipe)

For pasta: Drop pasta into about 8 quarts boiling salted water. Boil rapidly until pasta is tender but still firm to the bite (al dente). Drain in colander, rinse with cold water and drain again. Transfer to large bowl. Add oil and vinegars and toss lightly. Season to taste with salt and pepper; toss again. Cover pasta and refrigerate until serving time.

For vegetables: Separately steam asparagus and broccoli just until crisp-tender; *do not overcook.* Rinse with cold water to stop cooking process and retain bright green color. Steam fresh peas in same manner; rinse with cold water. (Do not cook frozen peas.) Store in plastic bags in refrigerator.

Mince 6 green onions and halve cherry tomatoes. Transfer to small bowl and refrigerate. Rinse spinach leaves, discarding any that are bruised or wilted. Wrap in plastic and chill.

For seafood: If using sea scallops, cut in half. Gently poach scallops in water that is just below the boil until barely firm, about 2 minutes. Drain and rinse with cold water. Poach shrimp in their shells in same manner as scallops just until they turn pink and are firm but not rubbery. Rinse with cold water. Shell and devein shrimp (shells may be reserved for use in stocks); cut shrimp in half. Transfer seafood to another large bowl. Add oil, vinegars and garlic and toss.

To assemble: About 30 minutes before serving, arrange spinach leaves around outer edge of large platter (preferably white or clear glass to accentuate colorful salad). Gently toss pasta with vegetables and reserved green onion-tomato mixture. Arrange in center of platter with spinach leaves as border. Make well in center of pasta.

Drain seafood. Toss with remaining green onion and season to taste with salt and pepper. Mound in center of pasta. Serve with Basil Cream.

Basil Cream

Prepare one to two days ahead.

Makes about 3 cups

⅓ cup cider vinegar or white wine vinegar
2 tablespoons Dijon mustard
½ cup tightly packed fresh basil leaves* or 3 to 4 tablespoons dried basil, crumbled

1 to 2 large garlic cloves
⅓ cup vegetable oil
1 cup sour cream
½ cup whipping cream
3 tablespoons minced fresh parsley
Salt and freshly ground pepper

Combine vinegar, mustard, basil and garlic in processor or blender and mix until almost smooth. With machine running, drizzle in oil. Add sour cream, whipping cream and parsley and puree until smooth. Season to taste with salt and pepper. Refrigerate until shortly before serving. Stir through several times before pouring into serving bowl.

*If fresh basil is not available, increase parsley to 7 tablespoons to give sauce pale green tint.

Risotto con Frutti di Mare

The amounts of shellfish in this hearty risotto can be adjusted to suit your personal taste. And it could easily stand alone as a main dish, with salad and cheese to complete the meal.

4 servings

1½ tablespoons unsalted butter
1 medium onion, minced (about 1 cup)
12 ounces Arborio rice* (about 1½ cups)
⅓ cup dry white wine
3½ to 4½ cups chicken stock (preferably homemade and unsalted)
1½ tablespoons olive oil
6 small squid, cleaned, skinned and diced
2 tablespoons minced Italian parsley

2 garlic cloves, lightly crushed (about ½ teaspoon)
1 tablespoon minced fresh basil or ½ teaspoon dried, crumbled
1 medium-size dried medium-hot red chili, seeded and crumbled
1 pound mussels, scrubbed and debearded (about 1 dozen)
½ pound uncooked shelled small shrimp, (about 2 dozen)
2 tablespoons minced Italian parsley
Salt and freshly ground pepper

Melt butter in heavy 3- to 4-quart saucepan over medium-low heat. Add onion, cover and cook until soft and translucent, about 10 minutes (do not brown). Stir in rice. Increase heat slightly and cook until rice absorbs some of butter, about 3 minutes, stirring constantly. Add wine and stir until absorbed, about 1 minute. Add ½ cup stock and stir until rice is almost dry. Repeat with another ½ cup stock. *(Rice can be prepared ahead and set aside in cool place for up to 8 hours.)*

Heat olive oil in heavy 2-quart saucepan over medium-high heat. Stir in squid, parsley and garlic and sauté about 3 minutes. Add 1 cup stock with basil and red chili. Reduce heat, cover and simmer gently 30 minutes, adding small amount of stock if necessary. Add mussels, cover and cook until shells open, 5 to 10 minutes; discard any mussels that do not open. Set aside to cool. Remove mussel shells and discard. Return mussels to pan. Stir in shrimp. Refrigerate until ready to use.

Bring remaining stock to boil. Warm rice mixture over medium heat. Increase heat to medium high, add about ½ cup hot stock and stir until liquid is absorbed. Repeat with another ½ cup stock. Taste rice (it should be firm but tender). If rice if too firm, add small amount of stock and cook until liquid is absorbed. Add entire fish mixture and cook until liquid is absorbed and rice is creamy, stirring constantly. Stir in parsley. Season with salt and pepper.

* Available in specialty food stores.

Marseilles-Style Grilled Skewers of Shrimp, Scallop and Squid

Succulent fish threaded between slices of fresh lemon, bay leaves and orange, and basted with red pepper–flavored olive oil during grilling.

12 servings

1 cup olive oil
1 teaspoon dried red pepper flakes
3 garlic cloves

12 thin small lemon wedges
12 uncooked prawns, shelled and deveined
6 slices bacon, blanched 3 minutes in boiling water, drained and halved
12 sea scallops
12 small bay leaves, soaked in water 1 hour
6 medium squid, cleaned and halved lengthwise to form flat pieces

6 small thin orange slices, halved

Sage-Lemon Butter
½ cup (1 stick) butter
1 tablespoon fresh lemon juice
1 teaspoon dried sage leaves, crumbled
Grated peel of ¼ medium lemon

½ cup coarse fresh breadcrumbs
Grated peel of ½ medium lemon

Italian parsley sprigs (garnish)

Combine olive oil, red pepper flakes and garlic in bowl. Set aside 2 hours.

Thread the following onto each of twelve 9- to 10-inch skewers in order given: 1 lemon wedge, 1 prawn, ½ bacon slice (rolled up), 1 scallop, 1 bay leaf, 1 piece of squid and 1 orange slice. Refrigerate skewers until ready to grill.

For butter: Melt butter in small saucepan. Whisk in lemon juice, sage and grated lemon peel. Set aside.

Prepare charcoal grill or preheat broiler. Grill skewers close to heat source until shrimp are pink, 6 to 8 minutes, brushing frequently with flavored olive oil and sprinkling breadcrumbs over during last 3 minutes. Spoon sage-lemon butter over skewers. Transfer to serving platter. Sprinkle with grated lemon peel. Garnish platter with parsley sprigs and serve.

Shellfish Sausage (Boudins de Fruits de Mer)

As its name implies, this is a puree of shellfish formed into the elongated shape of a sausage. The fish should be as fresh as possible so that it has texture and enough albumin to hold the cream. Frozen thawed fillets will cause the mixture to bleed or separate. If "wharf-fresh" fish is not available in your area, add an egg white to the sole before pureeing. Since real sausage casings can be hard to find and delicate to work with, you can mold the sausage in foil, allowing for easier handling and more flexibility in determining the final size and shape. The boudins may be prepared a day ahead, kept in foil and chilled until ready to serve, and then reheated in hot (not boiling) water. Serve with poached, lightly salted cucumbers or tiny boiled potatoes.

8 luncheon or 16 appetizer servings

Boudins
½ pound unshelled raw shrimp
1 pound sole fillets (preferably gray, lemon or petrale), trimmed and cut into ½-inch pieces
1 egg white (optional)
1½ cups whipping cream
1 tablespoon minced mixed *fresh* herbs (such as tarragon, parsley, chives)
½ pound scallops, cut into ¼-inch pieces
1 teaspoon salt
¼ teaspoon freshly ground white pepper

Sauce
1 pint shucked oysters, undrained
½ cup white wine
1 cup fish trimmings
3 cups Fish Fumet (see recipe, page 72) *or* water
¾ cup thinly sliced onion
½ cup dry Sherry
½ cup celery leaves
1 bay leaf
½ teaspoon crushed black peppercorns
½ teaspoon salt
¼ teaspoon dried thyme leaves
¾ cup (1½ sticks) unsalted butter, cut into pieces

For boudins: Generously butter 3 large pieces of aluminum foil (each about 14 inches long) for casings; set aside.

Peel shrimp (reserve shells for sauce) and cut into ½-inch pieces; set aside.

Puree sole several seconds in processor or blender (add egg white if necessary). Stop machine to scrape down sides of bowl and continuing mixture until puree is smooth. Add ½ cup cream and blend several seconds more.

Whip remaining cream in large bowl until slightly thickened. Add herbs and blend well. Whisk in puree. Fold in shrimp, scallops, salt and pepper.

Spoon ⅓ of fish mixture into each piece of foil and roll to enclose. Twist ends tightly to seal. Place "sausages" in large skillet and cover with cold water. Set small lid over sausages to weight down and keep immersed. Cover with regular lid, bring water to 180°F and cook about 15 minutes. *Do not boil; water should just be shivering, not even simmering.* Remove from heat and let sausages stay in water about 10 minutes.

Remove sausages from water and unwrap carefully. Discard any accumulated liquid. Transfer to buttered dish, cover with waxed paper and keep warm in 160°F oven while preparing sauce.

For sauce: Combine oysters, oyster liquid and wine in skillet and bring to simmer. Poach gently until oysters are firm. Strain and reserve liquid. Keep oysters warm while completing sauce.

Puree reserved shrimp shells in processor or blender. Transfer to saucepan and add fish trimmings, reserved liquid from poaching oysters, fish fumet, onion, Sherry, celery leaves and seasonings. Place over medium heat and bring to boil. Boil gently 20 to 25 minutes.

Strain. Return liquid to saucepan and reduce to approximately ½ cup. Reduce heat to low and add butter piece by piece, beating well after each addition. Taste and adjust seasoning if needed. Coat sausages with sauce, garnish with oysters and serve immediately.

If preferred, smaller boudins may be made. Adjust cooking time accordingly.

Steamed Fish with Sauce

6 to 8 servings

1 1½- to 3-pound whole fish (size will depend on availability), cleaned (head and tail left on)

3 tablespoons chicken stock
2 tablespoons steak sauce
2 tablespoons light soy sauce
2 tablespoons oyster sauce
2 tablespoons minced fresh garlic
2 tablespoons minced green onion

1 tablespoon finely grated fresh ginger
1 tablespoon bean sauce*
1 tablespoon hoisin sauce
1 teaspoon sugar

1 tablespoon oil

¼ to ½ cup slivered green onion (garnish)

Make 3 diagonal slashes on each side of fish. Steam fish until done (allow 10 minutes for each 1 inch thickness, measuring at thickest part of body). Transfer to serving platter.

Combine next 10 ingredients in small mixing bowl. Heat oil in wok or saucepan over medium-high heat. Add stock mixture and bring to boil. Pour over fish and garnish with green onion.

*Available in oriental markets.

Whole Baked Fish Dalmatian Style

4 servings

1 2- to 3-pound bass, bluefish, mullet or carp, cleaned
Salt

¾ cup olive oil
1 onion, minced
1½ cups cooked rice
Juice of ½ lemon

2 garlic cloves, minced
Paprika
Salt and freshly ground pepper
Chopped fresh parsley

1 cup cornmeal
1 to 2 teaspoons paprika
Brandy (optional)

Preheat oven to 350°F. Lightly oil baking dish. Lightly rub fish skin with salt.

Heat oil in large skillet over medium heat. Add onion and sauté until translucent. Add rice, lemon juice and garlic and cook 5 minutes, stirring frequently. Add paprika, salt, pepper and chopped parsley and blend well. Stuff fish and sew opening with string.

Combine cornmeal and paprika on waxed paper. Use to coat fish completely. Place in baking dish and bake 15 minutes. Turn and continue baking until golden brown, about 10 minutes. Sprinkle with additional paprika. For a special touch, heat brandy, pour over fish and flambé it at the table.

Fish Mousse with Fennel Butter Sauce (Bavarois de Poisson)

8 servings

2 cups full-flavored Fish Fumet (see recipe, page 72)
1 teaspoon fennel seed

½ pound pike, sole or flounder fillets, skinned and boned
2 teaspoons unflavored gelatin

2 cups whipping cream
1 teaspoon salt

Lettuce leaves
Beurre Blanc Fennel Sauce (see following recipe)

Line bottoms of eight ¾-cup ramekins or soufflé dishes with parchment paper; butter paper. Set dishes aside.

Bring fish fumet and fennel seed to boil in medium saucepan over medium-high heat. Boil 3 minutes. Let cool to room temperature.

Strain mixture into medium saucepan. Stir in fish and gelatin and cook over medium-high heat until mixture is reduced by ⅓ and fish flakes easily, about 3 to 5 minutes. Transfer mixture to processor or blender and puree about 3 minutes. Transfer puree to large bowl. Set in large bowl filled with ice cubes, stirring puree constantly until room temperature. Remove bowl from ice bath and set aside.

Combine cream and salt in medium bowl and beat until soft peaks form. Fold whipped cream into puree. Spoon mixture evenly into prepared dishes or ramekins. Refrigerate overnight.

Arrange lettuce leaves on 8 salad plates. Unmold each serving into center of each plate. Gently remove parchment paper. Spoon sauce over each mousse and serve immediately.

Beurre Blanc Fennel Sauce

Makes ½ cup

6 black peppercorns	1 large shallot, chopped
2 tablespoons fennel vinegar*	½ cup (1 stick) well-chilled butter,
2 tablespoons dry vermouth	cut into 16 pieces

Combine peppercorns, fennel vinegar, vermouth and shallot in small heavy saucepan and cook over medium-high heat until reduced to glaze, about 3 to 5 minutes. Remove pan from heat. Whisk in 2 pieces butter 1 piece at a time and stir until mixture is smooth. Place pan over low heat and whisk in remaining butter in same manner. Serve immediately.

*For fennel vinegar, combine ¼ cup white wine vinegar and 1 teaspoon fennel seed in small saucepan and bring to simmer over medium heat. Let simmer 5 minutes. Strain vinegar thoroughly before using.

Shrimp and Scallop Curry

Serve over rice.

6 to 8 servings

36 uncooked medium shrimp, peeled and deveined (shells reserved)	1 pound scallops
	Salt and freshly ground pepper
2 green onions, minced	Curry powder to taste
2 garlic cloves, minced	1 tablespoon clarified butter
Curry powder to taste	1 tablespoon chopped fresh parsley
3 cups whipping cream	
1 cup dry white wine	

Combine shells, green onion, garlic and curry powder in medium skillet over medium-high heat and sauté about 1 minute. Blend in cream and wine. Increase heat to high and cook, stirring constantly, until sauce is thick, about 5 minutes. Remove from heat. Discard shells using slotted spoon. Set cream sauce aside.

Season shrimp and scallops with salt, pepper and curry powder. Heat butter in heavy medium saucepan over medium-high heat. Add shrimp and scallops in batches and sauté 2 minutes. Remove with slotted spoon and set aside. Add cream sauce to same saucepan and cook until sauce is thick, about 2 to 3 minutes. Return shrimp and scallops to saucepan. Blend in chopped fresh parsley. Serve immediately.

Mussel and Shrimp Pilaf

6 servings

1 cup basmati rice* or long-grain white rice

3 pounds mussels or 20 small clams
½ cup dry white wine
½ cup water

1 pound uncooked shrimp, peeled and deveined
3 tablespoons minced fresh cilantro (also known as coriander or Chinese parsley)

1 cup (or more) tomato juice
3 tablespoons fresh lemon juice
1 teaspoon salt
¼ teaspoon freshly ground white pepper
Finely grated peel of 1 lemon

6 tablespoons (¾ stick) butter
2 cups thinly sliced onions
2 medium garlic cloves, minced
¼ teaspoon salt

If using basmati rice, place in strainer and rinse under cold running water, removing any foreign particles. Cover rice with water and let stand for about 15 minutes. Drain and rinse again. Drain thoroughly and set aside.

Scrub mussels or clams well under cold running water. Bring wine and water to boil in large heavy saucepan or Dutch oven over medium-high heat. Add mussels hinge side down. Cover and steam until mussel shells have opened, about 5 to 10 minutes.

Ladle mussels into bowl, discarding any unopened shells; reserve cooking liquid. Remove mussels from shells, reserving liquid. Rinse mussels under cold water, removing any remaining hairlike substances. Combine shrimp, cilantro and mussels in large bowl.

Strain all reserved liquid through 3 thicknesses of cheesecloth. Measure; add enough tomato juice to make 2 cups. Add lemon juice, salt, pepper and lemon peel. Set aside.

Melt butter in 4-quart heavy saucepan over low heat. Add onion, cover and cook about 5 minutes. Uncover and cook until onion is soft and golden, about 10 minutes. Add garlic, rice and salt. Increase heat to medium and cook, stirring constantly, about 2 minutes. Add tomato-mussel liquid and bring to boil. Reduce heat and simmer about 15 minutes, stirring mixture occasionally.

Arrange mussels and shrimp over rice. Cover and steam until shrimp are pink and rice is cooked through, about 7 minutes. Stir through several times. Taste and adjust seasoning. Turn into dish and serve immediately.

*Available in Indian food stores.

Green and White Seafood Pilaf

8 servings

4 cups Seafood Stock (see following recipe)
2 cups converted rice
4 to 5 small zucchini, cut into 2 × ½-inch julienne (4 cups)
2 cups coarsely chopped broccoli *or* asparagus
2 dozen littleneck clams, scrubbed
1 10-ounce package frozen peas

2 pounds uncooked shelled large shrimp (2¼ pounds unshelled)
2 pounds whole bay scallops or quartered sea scallops
40 small snow peas

4 large green onions, minced (garnish)
Freshly ground pepper

Bring Seafood Stock to boil in 6- to 8-quart paella pan or deep heavy skillet over medium-high heat. Stir in rice, cover and cook 5 minutes. Add zucchini, broccoli and clams (hinged sides down). Cover and cook 7 minutes. Quickly add frozen peas; top with shrimp, scallops and snow peas. Cover and continue cooking until rice is tender and seafood and vegetables are cooked, about 3 minutes. If any liquid remains in bottom of pan, increase heat to high and cook briefly uncovered until all liquid is absorbed. Remove from heat and sprinkle with green onion. Serve directly from pan, seasoning with pepper at table.

Seafood Stock

Makes 4 cups

½ cup olive oil
2 cups sliced onion
1 cup diced red or green bell pepper or combination
1 tablespoon minced garlic
2 cups chicken stock (preferably homemade)
2 cups clam juice

1 cup dry white wine
4 ¼-inch-thick lemon slices
2 bay leaves
1 teaspoon dried thyme leaves, crumbled
1 teaspoon fennel seed
½ teaspoon ground coriander
½ teaspoon dried red pepper flakes

Heat oil in large paella pan or deep heavy skillet over medium-high heat. Add onion, bell pepper and garlic and sauté until onion and garlic are golden, about 12 minutes. Stir in all remaining ingredients and bring to boil. Let boil until reduced to 4 cups. Discard lemon and bay leaves. Use stock immediately or refrigerate up to 2 days.

Panache of Salmon and Turbot in Sweet Pepper Butter

One of the delightful dishes from chef-owner Michel Lorain of A la Côte St.-Jacques in Joigny, near Chablis.

4 servings

1 ¾-pound turbot fillet
1 ¾-pound salmon fillet
Salt and freshly ground pepper

1 large red bell pepper

6 tablespoons plus 2 teaspoons dry white wine
3 tablespoons plus 1 teaspoon white wine vinegar

1 tablespoon minced shallot
2 tablespoons crème fraîche
11 tablespoons unsalted butter, cut into ½-inch pieces

Fresh chervil leaves (garnish)

Lightly butter 2 baking sheets. Holding knife at slight angle, cut turbot and salmon fillets crosswise into ½-inch-thick slices, forming even medallions. Season both sides with salt and pepper. Arrange turbot and salmon on separate baking sheets.

Preheat broiler. Place bell pepper in broiler pan. Roast 6 inches from heat source, turning until blackened on all sides. Transfer to plastic bag. Set aside 10 minutes to steam. Peel pepper, discarding veins and seeds. Rinse, if necessary, and pat dry with paper towels. Cut half of pepper into fine julienne; set aside for garnish. Press remaining half through fine strainer to puree.

Combine wine, vinegar and shallot in heavy medium saucepan over medium-high heat and cook until liquid is reduced to 2 tablespoons. Blend in crème fraîche and heat through. Reduce heat to low and whisk in butter 1 piece at a time. *(If at any time sauce begins to break down and separate, remove from heat and whisk in 2 pieces of butter.)* Blend in pepper puree. Season with salt and pepper.

Preheat broiler. Broil fish separately until top is opaque, 2 to 3 minutes. Alternate turbot and salmon medallions cooked side down on large broilerproof platter. Pour sauce over. Broil until fish is cooked through, about 2 minutes. Garnish with reserved pepper strips and chervil. Serve immediately.

❧ Index

Albacore Pâté, Smoked, 78
Antipasti, Mixed, 83

Bacon-Wrapped Scallops, 44
Bass. *See* Sea Bass; Striped Bass
Benihana, Shrimp, 19
Bluefish, Whole Baked, Dalmatian
   Style, 111
Boudins de Fruits de Mer, 110
Brandade de Morue, 79
Broth (Fish). *See* Stock
Butters. *See* Sauces

Calamari Vinaigrette, 54
Calistoga Inn's Fettuccini with
   Smoked Salmon, 92
Capered Swordfish Steaks, 76
Capesante, 49
Carp, Whole Baked, Dalmatian
   Style, 111
Catfish, Crisp-Fried, 100
Ceviche, 68
Cheese and Shrimp Quiche with
   Mushrooms, 22
Chutney Shrimp on Shells of Pastry,
   11
Clam(s)
   Geoduck Stew, 32
   Gourmet, 30
   Green and White Seafood Pilaf,
     113
   Pavarotti, 31
   Steamed, Cosmo's, 31
   Steamed Littleneck, in Black Bean
     Sauce, 30
   Stuffed, 30
Codfish
   Geoduck Stew, 32
   Mousse, 79
   Sweet and Sour Fish, 82
Conch Fritters with Hot Sauce, 54
Coquilles St. Jacques. *See* Scallops
Court Bouillon, 75, 89, 98

Crab(s)
   in Black Bean Sauce, 7
   Cakes, Maryland Eastern Shore, 4
   Claws, Sautéed, 5
   Deviled, 3
   Dungeness, Umberto's, 2
   Jockey, Baked, 5
   Puffs Supreme, 2
   Ramekins Fruits de Mer, 26
   Rangoon, 3
   Sandwich, Hot, 6
   Seafood Cream Curry, 28
   Seafood in Phyllo, 27
   and Shrimp Piquant, 27
   Stew, Dockside Murphy's
     Maryland, 7
   Stuffed, 3
   Terrine of, and Fresh Vegetables,
     4
Crackly Crusted Sea Bass with
   Herbs, 58
Crisp-Fried Catfish, 100
Crocked Shrimp and Cheese with
   Cucumber Rounds, 9
Curried Herring, 81
Curried Oysters in Puff Pastry, 40
Curry, Seafood Cream, 28
Curry, Shrimp and Scallop, 112
Curry, Shrimp Korma, 21

Dalmatian Fish Stew, 100
Deviled Crab, 3
Dockside Murphy's Maryland Crab
   Stew, 7
Dressings. *See* Sauces
Duxelles, 65

Easy Scampi, 17

Feuilletés of Mussels la Napoule, 38
Fillet of Sole. *See* Sole Fillets
Fish. *See also* Seafood; Individual
   Names
   Baked, Mozzarella, 84

Balls with Snow Peas and
   Asparagus, 103
with Coriander Sauce, 99
Fumet, 6, 50, 62, 72
Fumet, Lean, 33
Microwave Tips and Techniques
   for Cooking, 97
Mousse with Fennel Butter Sauce,
   111
Poached, 74
Poaching, 74–75
Raw, Marinated Hilton Harbour
   Castle, 106
Steamed with Sauce, 111
Stew, Dalmatian, 100
Sweet and Sour, 82
Timbales with Oyster Sauce, 102
Whole Baked, Dalmatian Style,
   111
Five Flavor Shrimp with Candied
   Walnuts, 15
Florentine, Stuffed Sole, 72
Flounder
   Baked Fish Mozzarella, 84
   Mousse with Fennel Butter Sauce,
     111
   with Shrimp Sauce, 79
   Stuffed, 80
Fruits de Mer, Boudins de, 110
Fruits de Mer, Ramekins, 26
Frutti di Mare, Risotto con, 108

Gabby Crabby (Hot Crab
   Sandwich), 6
Garam Masala, 22, 36
Geoduck Stew, 32
Gingered Prawns, 17
Greek Shrimp, Simple, 18
Green and White Seafood Pilaf, 113
Gruene Mansion, 62

Haitian Lobster, 24
Halibut with Saké, Soy Sauce and
   Ginger, 81

Herring
 Curried, 81
 Sweet, 81
Hilton Harbour Castle Poissons
 Crus Marinés, 106

Jambalaya, Shrimp, 20

Lobster
 Haitian, 24
 Hot Sherried, in Brioche, 25
 Ragoût with Morels, 25
 Sauce, 65
 Stuffed Cabbage with Chive
  Butter, 23
Lomi Lomi Salmon, 87

Mackerel, Sweet and Sour Fish, 82
Malabar Mussels, 36
Marseilles-Style Grilled Skewers of
 Shrimp, Scallop and Squid, 109
Maryland Eastern Shore Crab
 Cakes, 4
Mayonnaise
 Green, 104
 Watercress, 48
Mediterranean Mussel Plaki, 34
Mediterranean Stir-Fry, 18
Microwave, Tips and Techniques
 for Fish, 97
Miramonte's Scallops à la Nage, 53
Monkfish with Spinach and
 Béarnaise Sauce, 82
Moules Marinière, 35
Mousse
 Fish with Fennel Butter Sauce,
  111
 Salmon, 87
 Shrimp, with Sauce Nantua, 12
 Shrimp, Scallop and Sole, 102
 Smoked Trout, 95
 Zucchini, Scallops Set on a, 51
Mullet, Whole Baked Fish,
 Dalmatian Style, 111
Mussel(s)
 with Garlic in Wine Broth, 35
 Malabar, 36
 Mediterranean, Plaki, 34
 Moules Marinière, 35
 in Mustard Sauce, 37
 in Puff Pastry (Feuilletés la
  Napoule), 38
 Risotto con Frutti di Mare, 108
 Salad with Saffron, Warm, 36
 Shellfish with Red Pepper Sauce,
  55
 and Shrimp Pilaf, 113
 Soufflés, 34
 Steamed, with Basil and White
  Wine, 33

Oyster(s)
 Baked, 42
 Broiled, 39

in Cream, 41
Curried, in Puff Pastry, 40
Dressing, 40
Grilled, with Ginger Lime
 Dressing, 39
Rarebit, 41
Sauce, 102, 110
Toscanini, 42

Panache of Salmon and Turbot in
 Sweet Pepper Butter, 114
Pan Dorato, 19
Papillote of Sea Bass with Tomato
 Fondue, 59
Pasta Primavera Salad with Seafood
 and Basil Cream, 107
Pastry, Classic Puff, 38
 Mussels in, 38
 Oysters, Curried in, 40
Pastry Shells, 11
Pâté, Smoked Albacore, 78
Peasant Shrimp, 13
Pickled Shrimp, Carolina, 9
Pike Mousse with Fennel Butter
 Sauce, 111
Plantation Gardens Red Snapper, 63
Pompano au Gros Sel, Sauce Noilly,
 83
Portuguese Tuna, 78
Prawns. See also Shrimp
 Baked with Garlic and Herbs, 16
 Gingered, 17
Puff Pastry, Classic, 38

Quiche, Cheese and Shrimp, with
 Mushrooms, 22

Ragoût of Lobster with Morels, 25
Ramekins Fruits de Mer, 26
Rarebit, Oyster, 41
Red Snapper
 in Cognac-Parmesan Sauce, 63
 en Croûte with Lobster Sauce, 65
 Fillets, with Herbs, 62
 Gruene Mansion, 62
 Plantation Gardens, 63
 Poached, with Avocado Sauce,
  Cold, 60
 Suprême of, Duglère, 61
 Szechwan, 64
Rice
 Cinnamon, 28
 Indian, 22
Risotto con Frutti di Mare, 108
Rye Heart Toast, 96

Salad(s)
 Mussel, with Saffron, Warm, 36
 Pasta Primavera, with Seafood
  and Basil Cream, 107
 Scallops with Grapefruit, 43
 Shrimp, 14
 Shrimp and Carnation, 13

Shrimp in Cucumber Nests with
 Dill Dressing, 14
Squid (Calamari Vinaigrette), 54
Squid, with Green Ginger Sauce,
 55
Salmon
 in Basil Sauce, 90
 Braised, in Lettuce, 88
 Lomi Lomi, 87
 Mousse, 87
 à la Nage with Beurre Rouge, 90
 Paupiette with Cucumber and
  Mint, 91
 Poached, Sauce St. Jacques, 88
 in Saffron and Basil Sabayon,
  Fresh, 86
 Slices in Leek Sauce, Fresh, 89
 Smoked, Calistoga Inn's Fettuccini
  with, 92
 Smoked, Tart, 92
 Smoked, Timbales with Sauce, 86
 and Turbot in Sweet Pepper
  Butter, Panache of, 114
Salmon Trout
 Fillets with Red Wine Sauce, 93
 Smoked, 94
 Soufflé with Sauternes and
  Ginger, 93
Sand Dabs with Grapefruit, Baked,
 84
Sandwich, Hot Crab, 6
Sardines, Mixed Antipasti, 83
Sauce(s)
 Basil Cream, 108
 Basil Sabayon, 86
 Béarnaise, 82
 Béarnaise, Blender, 104
 Béchamel, 32
 Beurre Blanc, 53
 Beurre Blanc Fennel, 112
 Beurre Rouge, 91
 Chive Butter, 23
 Chive, Rich, 11
 Dill Dressing, 14
 Ginger, Benihana of Tokyo, 19
 Ginger, Fresh, 67
 Ginger, Green, 55
 Ginger-Lime Dressing, 39
 Hollandaise, 6
 Hollandaise, Emerald, 45
 Horseradish, 95
 Leek, 89
 Lobster, 65
 Mayonnaise, Green, (Sauce
  Verte), 104
 Mayonnaise, Watercress, 48
 Moutarde au Citron, 37
 Mustard, Benihana of Tokyo, 20
 Mustard Dill, 104
 Nantua, 12
 Oyster, 102, 110
 Parsley Butter, 105
 Pimiento, 5
 Rémoulade, 105

Sage-Lemon Butter, 109
Shrimp Butter, 10
Spinach, 80
Tartare, 105
Tomato, 59, 96
Velouté de Poisson, 5
Scallop(s)
    Bacon-Wrapped, 44
    Baked Bay, 48
    Braised, in Champagne Sauce
        with Sliced Kiwi, 52
    Capesante, 49
    Cold Bay, 46
    with Grapefruit, 43
    Green and White Seafood Pilaf,
        113
    Grilled, with Rice Vinegar, 46
    Kebabs, 46
    Mousse, Shrimp, and Sole, 102
    on Mousse of Zucchini, 51
    à la Nage, Miramonte's, 53
    Pasta Primavera Salad with
        Seafood and Basil Cream, 107
    Poached, in Emerald Hollandaise,
        45
    Provençale with Pasta and
        Avocado, 53
    Saumon Poché Sauce St. Jacques,
        88
    Sauté, 48
    Sautéed, in Mustard Sauce, 52
    Seafood Boudin with Watercress
        Mayonnaise, 47
    Shanghai Velvet Sliced, 50
    Shellfish with Red Pepper Sauce,
        55
    Shellfish Sausage, 110
    and Shrimp Curry, 112
    Squid, and Shrimp, Marseilles-
        Style Grilled Skewers of, 109
    with Tarragon Herb Sauce, 49
    Timbales with Watercress Sauce,
        44
    Velouté de Coquilles St. Jacques
        et Artichauts, 49
    Vera Cruz, 52
Scampi. See also Shrimp
    alla Buongustaia, 18
    Easy, 17
Scrod Fillets with Spinach Cream,
    80
Sea Bass. See also Striped Bass
    Crackly Crusted, with Herbs, 58
    at Our Pleasure, 58
    Papillote of, with Tomato
        Fondue, 59
    Whole Baked Fish, Dalmatian
        Style, 111
Seafood. See also Individual Names
    Boudin with Watercress
        Mayonnaise, 47
    Cream Curry, 28
    in Phyllo, 27

Pilaf, Green and White, 113
    Stock, 114
Shellfish. See also Individual Names
    with Red Pepper Sauce, 55
    Sausage, 110
Shrimp
    l'Antiboise, Sauté of, 20
    Balls, Coconut, 8
    Benihana, 19
    Butter Sauce, 10
    and Carnation Salad, 13
    with Rich Chive Sauce, 11
    Chutney, on Shells of Pastry, 11
    Connoisseur, 18
    and Crab Piquant, 27
    Crocked, and Cheese with
        Cucumber Rounds, 9
    in Cucumber Nests with Dill
        Dressing, 14
    Curry, Korma, 21
    Curry, Seafood Cream, 28
    Easy Scampi, 17
    Etouffée, 17
    Fiji, 15
    Five Flavor, with Candied
        Walnuts, 15
    Greek, Simple, 18
    Green and White Seafood Pilaf,
        113
    Grilled, 16
    Grilled Skewers of, with Scallop
        and Squid, Marseilles-Style, 109
    Grilled in a Wrapper of Seaweed,
        16
    Jambalaya, 20
    LaMaze, 9
    Mediterranean Stir-Fry, 18
    Mousse with Sauce Nantua, 12
    Mousse, Scallop and Sole, 102
    and Mussel Pilaf, 113
    Peasant, 13
    Pickled, Carolina, 9
    Prawns, Baked with Garlic and
        Herbs, 16
    Prawns, Gingered, 17
    Quiche, with Cheese and
        Mushrooms, 22
    Ramekins Fruits de Mer, 26
    Risotto con Frutti di Mare, 108
    Salad, 14
    Salad, Pasta Primavera with
        Seafood and Basil Cream, 107
    Seafood in Phyllo, 27
    and Scallop Curry, 112
    Shellfish Sausage, 110
    Stock, 12
Smoked Albacore Pâté, 78
Smoked Salmon
    Calistoga Inn's Fettuccini with, 92
    Tart, 92
    Timbales with Sauce, 86
Smoked Salmon Trout, 94
Smoked Trout Mousse with Rye
    Heart Toast, 95
Snapper. See Red Snapper

Sole Fillet(s)
    Baked Fish Mozzarella, 84
    with Buttered Ginger Sauce, 67
    Ceviche, 68
    Double, Spinach Soufflé and
        Spinach Crêpe Paupiette, 70
    Fish Mousse with Fennel and
        Butter Sauce, 111
    Mousse, Shrimp and Scallop, 102
    with Mushrooms and Apples,
        Steamed in Paper, 69
    Oven-Poached, with Vegetables,
        68
    Poached, with Asparagus, 69
    Poached, Basic, 66
    Sautéed, with Fines Herbes, 66
    Sautéed, St. Tropez, 71
    Shellfish Sausage, 110
    Stuffed, Florentine, 72
    in Tarragon Butter, 67
    Wellington, 73
Soufflés, Mussel, 34
Soufflé, Salmon Trout with
    Sauternes and Ginger, 93
Soufflé, Sole Spinach, 70
Spinach-Stuffed Sole (Florentine), 72
Spinach-Stuffed Trout, 99
Squid
    Calamari Vinaigrette, 54
    Salad with Green Ginger Sauce,
        55
    Shrimp, Scallop, Marseilles-Style,
        Grilled Skewers of, 109
Stew(s)
    Dalmatian Fish, 100
    Dockside Murphy's Maryland
        Crab, 7
    Geoduck, 32
Stir-Fry, Mediterranean, 18
Stock
    Court Bouillon, 75, 89, 98
    Fish Fumet, 6, 50, 62, 72
    Fumet, Lean, 33
    Seafood, 114
    Shrimp, 12
    Vegetable, 45
Striped Bass
    Livornese, 59
    Snapper in Cognac-Parmesan
        Sauce, 63
Sweet and Sour Fish, 82
Swordfish
    Grilled, Zesty, 77
    Provençal, 77
    Steaks, Capered, 76
    Steaks with Lemon and Capers,
        76
Szechwan, Red Snapper, 64

Tapenade, Tuna and Watercress, 78
Tempura, 106
Terrine of Crab and Fresh
    Vegetables, 4
Timbales, Scallop, with Watercress
    Sauce, 44

Tortelloni, Green Stuffed with
   Trout, 96
Trout
   Green Tortelloni Stuffed with, 96
   Poached, with Saffron Butter
      Sauce, 98
   Pampano au Gros Sel, Sauce
      Noilly, 83
   Smoked Mousse with Rye Heart
      Toast, 95

Spinach-Stuffed, 99
Tuna
   Portuguese, 78
   Smoked Albacore Pâté, 78
   and Watercress Tapenade, 78
Turbot and Salmon, Panache of, in
   Sweet Pepper Butter, 114

Umberto's Dungeness Crab, 2

Vegetable Stock, 45
Velouté de Coquilles St. Jacques et
   Artichauts, 49
Velouté de Poisson, 5

Wellington, Sole, 73
Whitefish, Dalmatian Fish Stew, 100

🍃 Credits and Acknowledgments

The following people contributed the recipes included in this book:

A la Côte St. Jacques, Joigny, France, Michel Lorain, chef-owner
Alana's Texas Cafe, Austin, Texas
Aldo's Ristorante Trattoria, Portland, Oregon
Charles Allenson
Bob Arganbright
Aubergine, Munich, Germany, Eckhart Witzigman, chef-owner
August Moon Restaurant, Dallas, Texas
Margot Bachman
The Back Porch Cafe, Rehoboth Beach, Delaware
Susan Baerwald
Melissa Smith Baker
Terry Bell
Benihana of Tokyo, New York, New York
Bernard's, Los Angeles, California, Bernard Jacoupy, owner; Roland Gibert, executive chef
Blu Adriatico, Flushing, New York
Jennifer Brennan
Biba Caggiano
Calistoga Inn, Calistoga, California
Anna Teresa Callen
Chez Ernest, Victoria, British Columbia, Canada
Cecilia Chiang
Mary Beth Clark
Elyn and Phil Clarkson
Norma Clipperton
Cosmo's Underground, Las Vegas, Nevada
Déjà-Vu, Philadelphia, Pennsylvania, Salomon Montezinos, chef-owner
Lucille DeLucena
Des Moines Golf and Country Club, Des Moines, Iowa
Dockside Murphy's, Salisbury, Maryland
The Dolphin Inn, Taylors Point, Buzzards Bay, Massachusetts
Alain Dutournier
Robert Ehrman and Ray Henderson
Ernie's, San Francisco, California, Jacky Robert, chef; Victor and Roland Gotti, owners
Rodney Eubanks
Claudia Feury
Michel Fitoussi's Palace, New York, New York, Michel Fitoussi, chef-owner
Four Seasons Hotel, Washington, D.C.
Robert and Shelley Friedman and Ken and Phyllis Nobel
Linda Gates
Marion Gorman
Freddi Greenberg
Greenery, Ogden, Vermont
Gail-Nancy Hirschele
Geoffrey Holder
Kirk Huffard
Bill Hughes
Hyatt Regency, Kansas City, Missouri
Roger Jaloux

Jay's Restaurant, Dayton, Ohio
The Jockey Club, Washington, D. C., Paul Delisle, director
Joel's, Sacramento, California
Jane Helsel Joseph
Madeleine Kamman
Lynne Kasper
Sandy Katz
Marlene Kellner
Kingston Harbour Yacht Club, Mount Prospect, Illinois
Margaret H. Koehler
Alma Lach
La Cantina, Vancouver, British Columbia, Canada
La Côte Basque, New York, New York, Jean-Jacques Rachou, chef-owner
La Mascotte French Restaurant, Commack, New York
Louise Lamensdorf and Rene Steves
La Rive, Catskills, New York, René and Paulette Macary, owners
La Rotisserie du Chambertin, Gevrey-Chambertin, France, Pierre and Céliene Menneveau, owners
La Toque, Los Angeles, California, Ken Frank, chef
Rita Leinwand
L'Espérance, Saint-Père-sous-Vézelay, France, Marc Meneau, chef-owner
Le St. Germain, Los Angeles, California
Faye Levy
Longfellow's, St. Michaels, Maryland, Thomas Pinto, owner
Frances Lorenzen
John Loring
Lun Kee Restaurant, Vancouver, British Columbia, Canada
Copeland Marks
Joel McCormick
Berenice McLaughlin
Perla Meyers
Mirabeau, Oakland, California
Miramonte Restaurant and Country Inn, St. Helena, California
Jinx and Jefferson Morgan
Lori Nadler
The New School's Cooking Center, New York, New York, Robert Posch, chef
Bach Ngo and Gloria Zimmerman
Nimble's, Lahaini, Maui, Hawaii
Judith Olney
Kathryn Pease
Plantation Gardens, Kauai, Hawaii
Plum Tree Cafe, Denver, Colorado, Kevin Downing, chef
Dahlia Ross
Sondra Rykoff
Saloon Restaurant, Philadelphia, Pennsylvania
Richard Sax
Carolyn Schneider
Patricia Scully
Edena Sheldon
Shucker's Restaurant, Olympic Hotel, Seattle, Washington
Elsie Silva
Leon Soniat

Spago, Los Angeles, California, Wolfgang Puck, chef-owner
The Spinnaker, Sausalito, California, Jacques Arpi, chef
Judy Stakee
Karyn Taylor
Barbara and Donald Tober
Doris Tobias
Francis Tong
Toronto Hilton Harbour Castle, Toronto, Canada, Rudolph Mack, chef
Jeremiah Tower
Trader Vic's, San Francisco, California, Victor Bergeron, owner
May Wong Trent
Michele Urvater
Jane Vogel
Maggie Waldron
Jan Weimer
Charles and Helen Wilson's l'Auberge, Wayne, Pennsylvania
Roland S. Wirth

Additional text was supplied by:

Anthony Dias Blue, *Wine With Seafood*
Rita Leinwand, *Poaching Fish, Classic Sauces for Fish*
Randy Levin, *Sashimi and Sushi*
Thelma Pressman, *Microwave Tips and Techniques for Fish*
Jan Stuebing, *A Traditional Clambake*

Special thanks to:

Marilou Vaughan,
    Editor, Bon Appétit
Bernard Rotondo,
    Art Director, Bon Appétit
William J. Garry,
    Managing Editor, Bon Appétit
Barbara Varnum,
    Articles Editor, Bon Appétit
Laurie Glenn Buckle,
    Associate Editor, Bon Appétit
Brenda Koplin,
    Copy Editor, Bon Appétit
Leslie A. Dame,
    Assistant Editor, Bon Appétit
Robin G. Richardson,
    Research Coordinator, Bon Appétit
Patrick R. Casey,
    Vice-President, Production, Knapp Communications Corporation
Anthony P. Iacono,
    Vice-President, Manufacturing, Knapp Communications Corporation
Philip Kaplan,
    Vice-President, Graphics, Knapp Communications Corporation
Donna Clipperton,
    Manager, Rights and Permissions, Knapp Communications Corporation
Karen Legier,
    Rights and Permissions Coordinator, Knapp Communications Corporation
Rose Grant
Sylvia Tidwell

The Knapp Press
is a wholly owned subsidiary of
KNAPP COMMUNICATIONS CORPORATION.
Chairman and Chief Executive Officer:
Cleon T. Knapp
President: H. Stephen Cranston
Senior Vice Presidents:
Rosalie Bruno *(New Venture
Development)*
Betsy Wood Knapp *(MIS Electronic
Media)*
Harry Myers *(Magazine Group
Publisher)*
William J. N. Porter *(Corporate Product
Sales)*
Paige Rense *(Editorial)*
L. James Wade, Jr. *(Finance)*

THE KNAPP PRESS

President: Alice Bandy; *Administrative
Assistant:* Beth Bell; *Editor:* Norman
Kolpas; *Managing Editor:* Pamela Mosher;
Associate Editors: Jan Koot, Sarah Lifton,
Diane Rossen Worthington; *Assistant
Editors:* Colleen Dunn Bates, Nancy D.
Roberts; *Department Assistant:* Teresa
Roupe; *Art Director:* Paula Schlosser;
Designer: Robin Murawski; *Book
Production Manager:* Larry Cooke; *Book
Production Coordinators:* Veronica
Losorelli, Joan Valentine; *Director,
Rosebud Books:* Robert Groag; *Creative
Director, Rosebud Books:* Jeff Book;
Financial Manager: Joseph Goodman;

Assistant Finance Manager: Kerri
Culbertson; *Financial Assistant:* Julie
Mason; *Fulfillment Services Manager:*
Virginia Parry; *Director of Public Relations:*
Jan B. Fox; *Marketing Assistants:* Dolores
Briqueleur, Randy Levin; *Promotions
Managers:* Joanne Denison, Nina Gerwin;
Special Sales Manager: Lynn Blocker;
Special Sales Coordinator: Amy Hershman

This book is set in Sabon, a face designed by Jan Teischold in 1967 and based on early
fonts engraved by Garamond and Granjon.

Composition was on the Mergenthaler Linotron 202 by Graphic Typesetting Service.

Series design by Paula Schlosser. Page layout by Renée Cossutta.
Project editor: Jan Stuebing

Color separations by NEC Incorporated.

Printing and binding by R.R. Donnelley and Sons.